EUROPEAN POLITICAL, ECONOMIC, AND SECURITY ISSUES

EUROPEAN UNION

POLITICAL, ECONOMIC AND SOCIAL ISSUES

EUROPEAN POLITICAL, ECONOMIC, AND SECURITY ISSUES

Additional books in this series can be found on Nova's website under the Series tab.

Additional e-books in this series can be found on Nova's website under the eBooks tab.

EUROPEAN POLITICAL, ECONOMIC, AND SECURITY ISSUES

EUROPEAN UNION

POLITICAL, ECONOMIC AND SOCIAL ISSUES

WILBERT STRICKLAND
EDITOR

nova
science publishers
New York

NOTICE TO THE READER

The Publisher has taken reasonable care in the preparation of this book, but makes no expressed or implied warranty of any kind and assumes no responsibility for any errors or omissions. No liability is assumed for incidental or consequential damages in connection with or arising out of information contained in this book. The Publisher shall not be liable for any special, consequential, or exemplary damages resulting, in whole or in part, from the readers' use of, or reliance upon, this material. Any parts of this book based on government reports are so indicated and copyright is claimed for those parts to the extent applicable to compilations of such works.

Independent verification should be sought for any data, advice or recommendations contained in this book. In addition, no responsibility is assumed by the publisher for any injury and/or damage to persons or property arising from any methods, products, instructions, ideas or otherwise contained in this publication.

This publication is designed to provide accurate and authoritative information with regard to the subject matter covered herein. It is sold with the clear understanding that the Publisher is not engaged in rendering legal or any other professional services. If legal or any other expert assistance is required, the services of a competent person should be sought. FROM A DECLARATION OF PARTICIPANTS JOINTLY ADOPTED BY A COMMITTEE OF THE AMERICAN BAR ASSOCIATION AND A COMMITTEE OF PUBLISHERS.

Additional color graphics may be available in the e-book version of this book.

Library of Congress Cataloging-in-Publication Data

ISBN: 978-1-53612-359-3

Published by Nova Science Publishers, Inc. † New York

CONTENTS

Preface		**vii**
Chapter 1	The European Union's Capitalism in Crisis *Noralv Veggeland*	**1**
Chapter 2	The Incapacity of the Union to Act as a Reliable Actor in the International Arena *David Ramiro Troitino, Archil Chochia and Tanel Kerikmäe*	**11**
Chapter 3	Online Piracy and Human Rights: Reflections on the European Approach *Anna G. Micara*	**33**
Chapter 4	Critics of the Catalan Independence Process and Catalan Political Nationalism *David Ramiro Troitino, Archil Chochia and Tanel Kerikmäe*	**77**
Index		**99**

PREFACE

In Europe, where the financial crisis was transformed into national debt crises in several countries, the current phase of the denial cycle marked by an official policy approach predicated on the assumption that normal restored through a mix of austerity, privatization and less state involvement came through (anti-Keynes). The other view is this. Governmental investments – and financial decision-making to regulate the effective demand in national economies is based on the basic principles introduced by John Maynard Keynes in his 'General Theory of Employment, Interest and Money (1936), The solution of the temporary crisis of the democratic capitalism might be linked to Keynes by his successors the neo-Keynesians. However, the representative democracy has become weak and fragmented, and under control of international powerful multinationals. The citizens not any longer look upon their national government as their representatives but as representatives for interest of foreign states and international organizations. Poor public politics and policies are what come out of it. The first chapter examines the European Union's capitalism in crisis. The second chapter of this book presents the weakness of the EU lying in its own foundation principals; its developments and its incapacity for transforming from a successful internal peace system into a reliable world power. The third chapter analyzes the case-law of the EU on measures to fight online piracy so as to shed light on whether the Court of Justice of the European Union struck a fair balance between intellectual property and human rights. Also, the case-law of the European Court of Human Rights is examined. The last chapter analyzes Spain's internal conflict over the breakaway intentions of a part of Catalonian society, going through different influential aspects such as history, ethnicity, language and culture; economy, the structure of the Spanish central government, the role of European Union and several other milestones in the main claims of the supporters of the independence for Catalonia.

Chapter 1 - In Europe, where the financial crisis was transformed into national debt crises in several countries, the current phase of the denial cycle marked by an official policy approach predicated on the assumption that normal restored through a mix of austerity, privatization and less state involvement came through (anti-Keynes). The other view is this. Governmental investments – and financial decision-making to regulate the effective demand in national economies is based on the basic principles introduced by John Maynard Keynes in his 'General Theory of Employment, Interest and Money (1936), The solution of the temporary crisis of the democratic capitalism might be linked to Keynes by his successors the neo-Keynesians. However, the representative democracy has become weak and fragmented, and under control of international powerful multinationals. The citizens not any longer look upon their national government as their representatives but as representatives for interest of foreign states and international organizations. Poor public politics and policies are what come out of it.

Chapter 2 - The European Union is a community founded by Western European states that historically had several armed confrontations in order to achieve world supremacy. The conflicts between France, Germany and United Kingdom, supported by their European and American allies led towards two devastating wars affecting almost all the planet. Nevertheless the end of the WWII meant the rise of two new world powers, the United States of America and the Soviet Union and the Western European states were losing influence in the world affairs. However the Europeans were still important in economic terms playing the role of a middle state in the world affairs dominated by the Cold War.

This research presents the weakness of the EU lying in its own foundation principals; its developments and its incapacity for transforming from a successful internal peace system into a reliable world power.

Chapter 3 - Online piracy is a widespread and worrisome phenomenon that affects the intellectual property holders' rights and that could have detrimental effects for the economy of a country. On the other hand, the enforcement of intellectual property rights may affect human rights such as freedom of expression or the right to protection of personal data. This article analyzes the case-law of the EU on measures to fight online piracy so as to shed light on whether the Court of Justice of the European Union struck a fair balance between intellectual property and human rights. Also, the case-law of the European Court of Human Rights will be examined. It will be shown that the reasoning based on the balancing fundamental rights did not lead to greater legitimacy of intellectual property yet and that, from a more general perspective, the EU is shaping a *sui generis* regime compared to international law. The need for more guidance at the EU and international level strongly emerges.

Chapter 4 - The article analyzes Spain's internal conflict over the breakaway intentions of a part of Catalonian society, going through different influential aspects such as history, ethnicity, language and culture; economy, the structure of the Spanish central government, the role of European Union and several other milestones in the main claims of the supporters of the independence for Catalonia. The research disputes the nationalistic idea through a unionist perspective, arguing the supranational character of the Spanish state. In addition the writing draws attention to the fact that there is distortion between the physical area influenced by Catalan culture and the much smaller region of the political movements supporting the independence.

In: European Union
Editor: Wilbert Strickland
ISBN: 978-1-53612-359-3

Chapter 1

THE EUROPEAN UNION'S CAPITALISM IN CRISIS

*Noralv Veggeland**
Public Policy, Inland Norway University of Applied Sciences,
Lillehammer, Norway

ABSTRACT

In Europe, where the financial crisis was transformed into national debt crises in several countries, the current phase of the denial cycle marked by an official policy approach predicated on the assumption that normal restored through a mix of austerity, privatization and less state involvement came through (anti-Keynes). The other view is this. Governmental investments – and financial decision-making to regulate the effective demand in national economies is based on the basic principles introduced by John Maynard Keynes in his 'General Theory of Employment, Interest and Money (1936), The solution of the temporary crisis of the democratic capitalism might be linked to Keynes by his successors the neo-Keynesians. However, the representative democracy has become weak and fragmented, and under control of international powerful multinationals. The citizens not any longer look upon their national government as their representatives but as representatives for

* E-mail: Noralv.veggeland@inn.no.

interest of foreign states and international organizations. Poor public politics and policies are what come out of it.

Keywords: Regulation, Keynesianism, financial crisis, poor politics

WHO GOVERN?

The political German scientist Wolfgang Streeck writes in the Le Monde Diplomatique, January 2012 that "Every day we read in the newspapers that the markets dictate what sovereign and democratic states can do and what they cannot do for their citizens. The consequence is that the citizens not any longer look upon their government as their representatives but as representatives for interest of foreign states and international organizations". This is a correct statement. It is not the market that directly dictates governments, that is what deregulation of markets does. There is a close relation between the development of the modern western regulatory state and the process of creating markets and correcting markets in terms of Giandomenico Majone's conceptualization of the regulatory state (Majone 1994, 1997, 2003). It is regulations to accomplish these goals, both nationally and internationally, that dictate governments. The European Union dictates the government of the member states. So does membership of the World Trade Organization (WTO). National impotence is the outcome of the huge amount of worldwide market agreements (Veggeland 2009).

USAs depth of state is more than about 2860 000 billion dollar in foreign loans, and President Donald Trump has additionally promised a gigantic investment program. If implemented on future infrastructure like roads and railways and walls, the loans certainly will increase dramatically. This program means new huge extra loans. Financial crisis and recession dominates the Western capitalism of our time. The crisis in the Euro-zone is evidently a grave blow to European integration, but intimately connected to the international financial crisis. The collapse of the national state finances understood as a manifestation of a fundamental mechanism in the capitalistic system, where un-balance and un-stability is the rule instead of the opposite. The Western democratic capitalism has in the year after the Second World War, went through three crises and conflicting phases, and is now going through a fourth one. For the EU, additionally, the Great Britain is getting out as a member state, Brexit, and the huge refugee problem generates a pressure, which is waiting for an expensive solution.

In Europe, where the financial crisis transformed into national debt crises in several countries, the current phase of the denial cycle marked by an official policy approach predicated on the assumption that normal restored through a mix of austerity, privatization and less state involvement came through (anti-Keynes). The claim is that advanced countries do not need to apply the standard toolkit used by emerging markets, including debt restructurings, higher inflation, capital controls, and significant financial repression. Advanced countries do not resort to such gimmicks, policymakers say. To do so would be to give up hard-earned credibility, thereby destabilizing expectations and throwing the economy into a future vicious circle. Although the view that advanced country financial crises are completely different, and therefore should be handled completely differently, has been a recurrent ideological refrain, notably in both the European sovereign debt crises and the U.S. subprime mortgage crisis, this view is at odds with the historical track record. In most advanced economies, based on Keynesianism, state intervention, debt restructuring or conversions, financial tools, and higher inflation have been integral parts of the resolution of significant debt overhangs.

The after war period of economic crises started with 1) the stagflation crisis of the 1970s. Afterward came 2) a public deficit crisis up, followed by 3) a privatized deficit crisis. Today the phase forth is ruling consisting of both 4) a public and a privatized deficit crisis, a combination crisis. Adequately three solution to crises has been tested out with conditional success, and a forth solution is by now implemented. What we know is that every one of the solutions of the crises using traditional tools has led up to the next following crisis (Veggeland (ed.) 2016.

The US economist, Raghuram G. Rajan, puts weight on the cultural aspect of the financial crisis, and figures out what he call 'Fault Lines'

(2010). He points out powerlessness and the absence of coherence in the US democratic capitalism. His explanation puts weight on the catastrophic development of economic and social inequality. Inequality occurring as a crisis in many Western countries, with the USA as the leading nation in that sense, We have mentioned the risky behavior of the banks and heavy private loan taking leading to the financial crisis, and Rajan relates this development to the situation in the USA. This behavior he looks upon as only the last step in the process we have described a process with a wrong course by political powerlessness in an environment of globalized and steady more uncoordinated world.

Justice as a cultural matter and the fact that the citizens believe the government as the guarantee for democracy is neglected. Rajan points out that for every single dollar in salary growth between 1976 and 2007 went 58% of that growth to the one richest percent of the families in USA. He continues to tell us that the income of the social middleclass and the poor labor class has stagnated or decreased, while the income of the richest 10% arose enormously. This development created a sort of disorder neglected by the politician, but obviously disturbed the legitimacy of the politics. Rajan shows that this dilemma got politicians to compensate for the occurrence of inequality and the threat to their legitimacy, by voting forward liberalization of the credit market and favoring consume financed by loan. He writes that politicians, always is sensible to their electorate, are choosing what they think as a solution of universal impact, namely to secure cheap loans to them suffering for not having participated in the growth of the economy and its outcome. The banks took the advantage of the situation to earn money of suspect real estate loans, namely subprime loan. The real estate market was for a while a hot spot in its function, realizing products to constantly higher prizes. People bought housing products characterized by steadily rising prizes, believing that the prizes would continue to rise – into heaven. High risk taken in this unregulated financial game. When the US Federal Reserve Bank let the interest on loan arise a bit, steadily more people were not able to upkeep their loans, i.e., pay part payment and interest rates. Accordingly, the banks shaken and threatened by going bankruptcy and did so. The Financial crisis spread worldwide after the 2007/2008.

The crisis that concerns the USA, EU and other Western countries is today what we might call a crisis of combination linked to both public and privatized loan and national budget deficits, for example look to Greek, Spain and Portugal. To get through this crisis the governments of these countries insist on budget cuts and saving programs, and cuts in salaries and pension arrangements. The impact of these actions is reduced market demand, which boosts the crisis in terms of rising unemployment. A natural consequence of this is social and political disturbance visible in many European countries. Wolfgang Streeck (2012) concludes: 'The crisis of today threatens the democratic order as much as the economic order, maybe even more'. As in the past, the crisis will find a provisional solution. Most likely, the crisis of combination this time will not favor the interests of speculative financial actors, which probably will become subordinated stronger international regulations, in Europe of the EU. (In the USA with the new President Trump with his buzzword "America First" nobody knows the way out.) The interests will remain, but expand their self in tight contact with the real capital, i.e., in contact with global industrial monopoly interests. Consequently, the citizens will to an even lower extent look upon their government and politicians as representatives and guaranty for democracy.

THE DEMOCRATIC CAPITALISM AND THE NEO-KEYNESIAN EXPLANATION ON THE CRISIS OF COMBINATION

Governmental investments – and financial decision-making to regulating the effective demand in national economies is based on the basic principles introduced by John Maynard Keynes in his 'General Theory of Employment, Interest and Money (1936), An explanation on the temporary crisis of the democratic capitalism linked to the Keynesian tradition must contain the following factors (Veggeland (ed.) 2016):

- Firstly, a central point in Keynesian theory was arguments for an active state whose main role was to correcting markets and to stabilizing economic circulations. – We have described and analyzed the stagflation crisis of the 1970s/80s and found that the state remained active. The Western governments chose comprehensive public loan taking and the issuing of government bonds, which later on got the consequence of a public crisis of credit.
- Secondly, by using the term 'inclination' to consume, Keynes was able to explain how the consumption behavior changed its character parallel to changing prizes in the market, in our case in the housing market. When the prizing of real estate rises, an inclination arises which generates a feeling of value gain, which turns into a feeling of saving money. Further on this turns into increasing consume because it is believed that the 'savings' are available right there. – This is the background for the development of what we have called the privatized credit crisis as a follower of the public credit crisis. The Government liberalized the financial markets, and the inclination to finance consume by loans increased. The inclination mostly created and inspired by the arising prizes in the housing market, and the false feeling of thereby saving money. When the housing bubble cracked, it became clear that the saving was not real.
- Thirdly, Keynes argued that financial melting down and the crack of aggregated demand in the economy closely related to upcoming inequality of income and stagnation in salary payments. The government compensated by liberalization of the financial policy and expanded its loan reserves in order to keep the welfare state going by redressing social problems with arrangements of support, guarantees and access to privatized loans. – What we call the crisis of combination does explain by this kind of Keynesian argumentation. While the net salary of 90 percent of the population changed very little during the last 20 years, the housing prizes have grown enormously in the same period. It is this reality that Rajan's

> 'Fault Lines' describes and analyzes. It is all about this. Selling real estate gave a surplus, which generated an inclination to higher consume in this market. Public and privatized crises of credit combined; public loan taking to pay welfare followed by a privatized crisis of credit. The EURO zone of the European Union (EU) hit by a crisis as a follower of the financial crisis. The EU, the European Central Bank (ECB) and the International Monetary Fund (IMF) chose a strategy to press national governments to cut welfare arrangements to prevent states to go bankruptcy; examples are what happen in countries like Greece, Spain, Portugal, Italy, Hungary and others. The privatized inclination to loan taking stopped by claiming a higher level of guarantee to get such loans.

We might describe the situation characterizing the Western democratic capitalism of today, involving three variables. High level of loan (Germany an exception) taking and aggregated consume generated a situation of low employment. During the crisis of combination of public and privatized credit crisis the unemployment rate will increase as time pass on. By necessity the inclination to public and private consume will be shrinking caused by mutual dependency between the variables. The inclination to the crackdown of aggregated demand and the growth of unemployment is strengthening by strong budget regulations and pay back of public loans. This situation occurred in the Euro-zone countries and hit them both economically and politically. In terms of Keynesian theory, the effective demand will decrease in the national economies. This triggers a negative economic spiral with growing unemployment followed by a corresponding decrease in purchasing power. When the national GNP begins decreasing it triggers printing of money, and the economies get threatened by increasing inflation. In the EU the European Central Bank (ECB) is very much aware of this mechanism, and keep on to implement a strong monetary policy in the Euro-zone. The other side of the coin is the grave impact of this policy on the Mediterranean countries already hit by the crisis of the capitalism. In the Eurozone, no one of its member states is allowed to devaluate its currency (Euro) in their endeavor to win more competitive ability in the world market. Low inflation rate makes loan does fall regarding nominal value. Consequently, the unemployment rate continues to rise followed by social and political disorder in the European countries mentioned. The crisis is most likely spreading to other countries as well.

Accordingly, a temporary respond in Europe seems to be on the one hand to increase the effective demand by import 1) capital from outside Europe to compensate for internal public loan taking. Such capital could come from the growing economies of the so-called BRICS countries, i.e., Brazil, Russia, India, China and South Africa. USA experiences a solution to the financial crisis by being a market for Chinese export whose payment remains as loan but with US dollar as involved currency in the business transactions. Regarding President Trump he has announced an end to this, and China will response in a way we so far do not know. 2) Dollar are printed and put into the money circulation, but inflation fails to appear because of US dollar as a global currency regarding economic transactions.

On the employment side might decreasing consume be avoided by giving the salaries of the labor force an upheaval. Increasing demand and consume will be an immediately output of the strategy, this deduced from the Keynesian analyses of inclination. The understanding of the combination crisis in the democratic capitalism is detained with a failure when it is explained as a crisis caused by an expensive welfare state together with public loans taken up to restore and pay for the services of the welfare state. Also the consideration of making the financial crisis part of the general housing policy and the political wish to make people owners of their own housing facilities is detained with failure. Rather, the explanation is to be found in the absence of Keynesian theory and its recommendation of governmental interventions when crisis hit the economic circulation in the capitalistic economy.

Shaping economic politics represents political choices. To go for a liberalized market economy generate consequences very much different compared to them generated by Keynesian strategies. The Nobel Prize winner in economy, Paul Krugman, has named the period between 1950 and 1972 "the period of compression (2007). The Keynesian principles dominated and pressed the market and the state together in a cooperative order. The unemployment was low and the inflation under control. Interventions of the government adjusted the market, and the building of the appreciated welfare state was the final outcome.

In contrast to this situation, Krugman says, that the period since 1980 characterized by divergence; the state has withdrawn from the marked and become a regulatory state, while the market forces were given freedom to develop and expand, only limited and in interplay with judicial regulations. The period characterized by high unemployment, but with inflation under control. This control came up due to the monetary political strategy whose main objective was fighting inflation. The salaries of ordinary people in the democratic capitalist countries went into a race to the bottom, and the trade unions lost power and influence in the economic and political games. This form of governance under former Prime Minister Margaret Thatcher in the UK and former President Ronald Reagan in the USA is well known.

Since the 1980s fragmentation of governance regimes has been a dominant development trend due to steering principles deduced from New Public Management theories. The representative democracy has become weak and fragmented and under control of international supranational citizens not any longer look upon their government as their representatives but as representatives for interest of foreign states and international organizations". Poor public politics and policies are what come out of it.

Two cases show that the people of Great Britain voted no stay as a member of the EU, and with Brexit as the consequence. The majority of the citizens wanted their country to be independent and national with benefits to the depth-dependent part of the people, caused by the foreign regulatory power of the EU. In the USA the people elected the rude businessman Donald Trump as their President with a hope that he could bring them better living conditions with his turn-around economic policies and turn to nationalism; "America first". The similarity between the two cases was the belief of the citizens that not any longer could the government be looked upon "as their representatives but as representatives for interest of foreign states and international organizations" – respectively UK the EU and USA China, Mexico and multinational trade agreements.

REFERENCES

Krugman, P. (2007), *The Conscience of a Liberal.* New York: W.W. Norton Company.

Majone, G. (1994), The rise of the regulatory state in Europe. *West European Politics, 17* (3), 77–101.

Majone, G. (1997), From the positive to the regulatory state: causes and consequences of change in the mode of government. *Journal of Public Policy, 17* (3), 139–89.

Majone, G. (2003), 'The Politics of Regulation and European Regulatory Institutions'. Op.cit. Hayward, J. and Menon, A. (eds.) (2003: 297-312).

Rajan, R. G. (2010), *Fault Lines: How Hidden Fractures Still Threaten the World Economy*. Princeton: Princeton University Press.

Streeck, W. (2012), *The Burden of Depth,* Le Monde Diplomatique Jan. 2012.

Veggeland, N. (2009), *Taming the regulatory state: Politics and ethics*, Cheltenham, UK and Northampton, MA, US: Edward Elgar Publishing.

Veggeland, N. (ed.) (2016), The Current Nordic Welfare Model, New York: Nova Science Publishers.

In: European Union
Editor: Wilbert Strickland
ISBN: 978-1-53612-359-3

Chapter 2

THE INCAPACITY OF THE UNION TO ACT AS A RELIABLE ACTOR IN THE INTERNATIONAL ARENA

David Ramiro Troitino, Archil Chochia and Tanel Kerikmäe
Tallinn University of Technology, Tallinn, Estonia

ABSTRACT

The European Union is a community founded by Western European states that historically had several armed confrontations in order to achieve world supremacy. The conflicts between France, Germany and United Kingdom, supported by their European and American allies led towards two devastating wars affecting almost all the planet. Nevertheless the end of the WWII meant the rise of two new world powers, the United States of America and the Soviet Union and the Western European states were losing influence in the world affairs. However the Europeans were still important in economic terms playing the role of a middle state in the world affairs dominated by the Cold War.

This research presents the weakness of the EU lying in its own foundation principals; its developments and its incapacity for transforming from a successful internal peace system into a reliable world power.

Keywords: European Union Foreign Affairs, European international relations, EU-Russia, empire of law, EU-US relations, world power, external action

INTRODUCTION

The methodology of this paper is based on the application of the different theories of integration to the most important events in the history of the European Union in foreign affairs. It provides useful information about how the Union reacts to external events under the influence of these theories, mainly Intergovernmentalism, Neofunctionalism and Federalism. Understanding the influence of these different ways of integration will provide with the necessary tools to develop a Foreign Policy according to the priorities of the Union.

The birth of the European Union can be traced to two tragically painful events, the World War II and the Cold War. Peace between the Western European States was a priority for the founding members because the material, political and social devastation consequence of the WWII could not be repeated again. Hence its main priority was avoiding future possible conflicts (Hadfield, 2014).

The key factor in order to endure peace were the relations between France and Germany, and subsequently the centre of the organization must be built on these two European countries. The Franco-Prussian war, the WWI and the WWII had generated a great animadversion the French and the German people, and had drag effect on the whole continent. Churchill in his famous speech in the University of Zurich (1946) pointed out the necessity to build a community including France and Germany as its centre, and UK patronizing it, to avoid new conflicts where UK could have been involved.

Hereafter, the Community including France and West Germany was designed as a peace system in order to prevent violent conflicts among its members. The external scope of the organization was to be conditioned by the Cold War and the international confrontation between two world giants, US and USSR. The full alignment of the Western European States with the North Americans meant counting with their troops deployed in the European soil for their defence (Nye, 1970).

The Cold War had another important effect on the creation of the first European Community and the further development towards the European Union. Western European states, with the outstanding exception of United Kingdom, had important internal social problems before and after the WWII. These social problems between lower social classes radicalized in anarchists, socialist and communist groups, and higher social classes affiliated to authoritarian political movements, were threatening the democratic system supported by the middle classes. The Spanish Civil War (1936-39) was a clear example of it, or the success of the Nazi party in Germany as a social stabilization against the threat of the then strong German communist party led by personalities as Ernst Thälmann or Werner Seelenbinder. The financial crisis of 1929 had weakened the position of the middle classes all over Europe as it affected the European economy destabilizing the political structures paving access of radicals to the pinnacle of power (Risse-Kappen, 1994).

At the end of the WWII the fascist forces were completely defeated in Europe with the irrelevant exception of Spain, but Communist was still a real political option as it was imposed over Central and East Europe by the Red Army. Also in Western Europe communism was an important player in the democratic states, as the French or Italian Communist parties proved, most of the Western European states counted with communist parties in their fragile democracies after the WWII with the exception of UK, the most stable political system of Europe and perhaps the world in the last centuries (Börzel, 2014).

The devastation generated by the years of war had affected negatively the European economy. A fast recovery was needed to avoid social instability that could foster the accession to power of national communist parties changing their alliance in the Cold War from US to USSR. The solution for the economic problems was the creation of a Common Market to raise trade between the member states and hence increase the economic activity of the national economies. Previously on this field the US led the successful Marshal Plan promoting the European economic recovery. The Americans also were involved patronizing the first European Community, the ECSC because Western Europe must be strong enough to face a hypothetical aggression from the Communist bloc. Henceforth the European Communities, ECSC and EEC, embryo of the current European Union, were designed as a peace system to avoid conflicts between France and Germany improving their cooperation and their economic performance to achieve social stability and override the internal threat of communism (Scott, 1998).

All the main targets included in the creation of the European Communities were internal without any active role in the external relations that were mainly left to the criteria of US, the main bastion of Western Europe against a Soviet aggression. During years the USSR perceived the European Communities just as an economic tool of the Western world led by US; a capitalist organization against the workers, against the self-proclaimed defender of the world workers, the Soviet Union. The neutral countries during the Cold War, as Sweden, Austria or Finland, could not join the European Communities because it would have broken their neutral status aligning with the Western World against the USSR (Hooghe, 2009).

The Role of US in Western Europe

Regardless the isolation of US after the WWI, the Americans took a leading international position after the WWII. World supremacy was not any longer a European dispute although since XVI century and the expansion of the Spanish and Portuguese empires, world hegemony was in European soil. The leading position of the commercial empire of the Netherlands, the British Empire, the French colonial system and the German challenge for world supremacy were different episodes of a European supremacy in the world politics.

At the end of the WWII the empires of UK and France still were spread all over the planet but rapidly disintegrated because of the incapacity of these metropolis controlling the oversee territories. Their weak position in economic, social and political terms made them incapable to face the internal unrest of their numerous colonies often foster by new international actors, as communism, as in the case of Vietnam where the French colonial forces could not defeat the local communist forces commanded by Ho Chi Minh. The withdrawal of France left an empty space occupied by US supporting actively the government of South Vietnam in its fight against the communist of the north.

The fierce competition between US and USSR subrogated the external relations of Western Europe to the necessities of the Cold War. The European interest was not the main priority as the communist threat was the main concern, a threat that could only be removed through the American leadership. The Suez crisis in the 56 generated by Egyptian unilateral nationalization of the Suez Channel, previously a property of joint British-French company, and a premium world communication route, unleashed a joint military action launched by Israel, France and UK. The operations were initially a success but the president of US, Dwight David Eisenhower, lobbied in favour of the Egyptians because the country was a key ally in the Arab world against the Soviet Union. The Europeans finally withdrawal fulfilling the American will against their own national interest.

The American predominance was also felt in the European soil as the country has military bases in Germany, Italy, United Kingdom, Spain, Belgium, Portugal, Greece and the Netherlands. Thousands of American soldiers were deployed in Western Europe becoming the main pillar of the Western European defence against any possible Soviet aggression. This predominance of US meant that the European Communities practically did not exist in terms of Foreign policy.

The Role of Neofunctionalism in the European Integration

The main scholar developing this theory of integration has been Ernst B. Haas, an American political scientist. Neo-Functionalism wants to replace power politics with a new supranational style following a clear strategy. First, areas of low politics, those that draw little attention from the public and the media, must be integrated. The importance is not given to high politics, such as a constitution or major areas as the military or a common political government, but economic areas that have to connect both needs and expectations of the member states, leaving aside those large issues as culture or defence that have a higher level of resistance from the social agents, media and national political actors (Mearsheimer, 1990).

The main personality leading the process of European integration, known as the father of Europe, was Jean Monnet. His involvement as main architect of the institutional framework of the European Communities was crucial developing the Union through a roadmap dominated by Neofunctionalism. His personal experience in the League of Nations, predecessor of United Nations, convinced him of the benefits of integration versus cooperation.

The main options for the European integration were, and to some extend still are, Federalism and Neofunctionalism. The first option is mainly political and it was opposed by nationalism because it meant fully integration between the members in the main fields, such as politics, economy or foreign relations. The idea was too advanced for the time and a much more modest approach was chosen for the European integration, Neofunctionalism, because it did not generated tensions and was based on a slow cautious development avoiding the conflictive areas.

Neofunctionalism focus on fields where the public interest is low, avoiding rejections or setbacks in the integration. It mainly started the integration in the economic field, planning thanks to the Spill-over effect to reach deeper integration in the future as a natural development of the process. The Schumann declaration, the official beginning of the European integration made clear the final target of the process, the creation of the United States of Europe. The Spill-over effect focus the process on areas with high potential for future integration as the benefits of the new fields under the common management will create a positive atmosphere for deeper integration. Likewise, the new integrated areas will in a medium or long term generate new problems, that can be solved with deeper integration or breaking at a high cost the previous steps. Hence deeper integration solves existing problems bringing new benefits to the community, but also creates new problems again solved with deeper integration (Troitiño, 2014).

The Neofunctionalism was a good option for the European necessities, peace and economic development because as more fields are integrated, the members share more aspects, and hence the possibilities of a conflict are highly reduced. Also the creation of a Common Market in different economic areas brought social stability to Western Europe. Clearly Neofunctionalism was a positive approach for Europe because of peace and social stability; foreign policy was not a priority (Ellingsen, 2000).

Other Theories Involves in the European Integration Process

At the beginning of the European integration the national governments did not want to lose the control over their sovereignty, giving it away to a political organization based on economic principals without any democratic control. Intergovernmentalism was the theoretical approach used to assure the control of the member states over the whole process of integration. Mainly this theory is based on cooperation versus integration, respecting the national independence on a free will community. This theory has influenced the European integration until nowadays and it is an important force inside the Union with a high capacity of influencing the European Union. Obviously this theory is based on the internal issues of the members of the community, respecting the independent behaviour of its members in the international arena, where they are going to act according to their national interest, and not according to the interest of the majority of the members of the organization and therefore it makes impossible to develop an effective common Foreign Affairs policy (Lavenex, 2004).

Federalism is the third pillar in terms of integration in the current European Union. Originally it did not have any major influence on the process but currently its importance is growing. Federalism draws a political roadmap integrating the main national institutions into a federal structure. In the case of Foreign Affairs, a common government leading the area with a strong and single voice abroad. The Federal Foreign Affairs will be focus on the necessities of the whole community and not in the particular situations of the member states. Hence any foreign action must lead to a general benefit for the majority of the community, even if it is against the national interest of a minority of the member states. Nevertheless the real impact of federalism in the current European Union is mainly in the internal decision-making influenced by the European Parliament, the field of Foreign Affairs is still a courtyard of Intergovernmentalism (Murdoch, 2004).

The European Defence Community and Its International Influence

During the 50's the support for integration in Western Europe was growing as a consequence of the success of the European Coal and Steel Community. The necessity of rearming military West Germany to face any violent aggression from the communist countries raised a strong social alarm in France. A new German army could lead to a new German aggression against France as revenge from the defeat of the WWII as previously had happened (Kerikmäe 2014). The solution proposed by the French National Assembly was the creation of a common European army including the new German forces and the armies of the rest of the members of the ECSC. Hence a Common Defence Community was proposed by France and eagerly accepted by the rest of the member states. Nevertheless France faced internal opposition to her own plan because there was a problem related with the political control of the new common army. The EDC was a military union based on a previous economic community without any major political aspects included in the common level. The new EDC must have taken the decision by unanimity, respecting the national sovereignty of the member states, becoming in reality the EDC in an ungovernable defence force. The solution was an Italian initiative, the

European Political Community, close to a federal idea, with common political institutions. Finally France rejected the idea and the EDC and the EPC were abandoned (Braudel, 1995).

The main consequence of the failure of the EDC was the inclusion of the new West German army in NATO, out of the European integration and under the guidance of US. The EDC could have been the embryo of a strong Foreign Policy in the European level through a common army managed by a common political entity. The final refusal of the French National Assembly in the mother of fact meant the predominance of Neofunctionalism in the European relations leaving aside sensitive issues as the European Army or a common Foreign Policy. National interest, national sovereignty was more important than foreign relations (Menon, 1992).

THE THIRD WAY OF DE GAULLE IN THE COLD WAR

The development of the European integration process after the EDC was highly influenced by Charles de Gaulle, president of France. The ideas of the French premier were in opposition to the acceptance inside Europe of the North American leadership in the field of defence and international relations. De Gaulle opposed the leading role of NATO, withdrawing France from the military aspects of the organization and moving away the headquarters of NATO out of French national soil (Sweet, 1997).

In the international arena de Gaulle tried to build a policy without the constrains of the Cold War, with for example official travels to the communist republic of Romania, or the Recognition of the People's Republic of China. Obviously he wanted to create a third way in the dual confrontation of the Cold War, he wanted to transform France in a world power restoring the glorious past of France in the world affairs. France acting alone because it lacked the human, economic and material resources to compete with US and the USSR in the international field could not achieve this ambitious plan. Hence de Gaulle focused on the European Communities looking forward the resources of its members to obtain a high international prestige for Europe, for France leading West Europe. Acting according to this political strategy de Gaulle presented a plan to reform the European Communities through Christian Fouchet, France's ambassador to Denmark. Basically the Fouchet plan pretended to change the own essence of the European communities because they were built as a peace system mainly following Neofunctionalism with important influences of Intergovernmentalism and minor contributions of federalism, and de Gaulle only contemplated one option, Intergovernmentalism. His reasons were clear according to his international policy designs, peace was not a concern because the Soviet Union was the external threat uniting the members of the European Communities, and hence Neofunctionalism was not an adequate vehicle for the relations of the members of the European organization. Intergovernmentalism also solved the problems raised by the EDC, because in the new community led by France the member states could then have kept intact their own popular sovereignty, their own separate armies, collaborating tightly together in the community level substituting the role of NATO as the European defender.

Nevertheless the rest of the members of the communities did not share the vision of de Gaulle, doubting about the lack of necessity of a peace system among them, and fearing the French leadership in the new community breaking the traditional balance of power inside the European Communities. Also, members of the Community under a direct threat of the Soviet Union, as West Germany, doubted about the French capacity to face a Soviet aggression in case of conflict. These led to the rejection of the Fouchet proposal but Intergovernmentalism increased its influence in the European Communities through the Luxembourg agreements (Pierson, 1996).

On the international politics, the refusal of the French proposal reduced de Gaulle's dream of a third way led by France to mere symbolic acts, keeping intact the dual supremacy of US and USSR with Western Europe as a weak dependant on US military forces, on American priorities and leadership through NATO in the foreign affairs relations.

The End of the Cold War and the New International Reality

The European Communities had successfully achieved its main objective of peace among its members and economic development to keep stable the political system of its members. It was a great triumph unparalleled in the history of mankind. This essence of the European communities was intact after the enlargement to most of Western Europe, including United Kingdom, Ireland, Denmark, Greece, Spain and Portugal, providing the same benefits to the new members: peace and social stability. But the end of the Cold War meant a new international situation as Soviet Union collapsed and Russia did not present any threat for the European states because of its internal situation.

The first consequence of the end of the Cold War was the German reunification and the inclusion of East Germany in the territory of the European Union, plus the enlargement to Austria, Finland and Sweden, previously neutral during the conflict. It was another important victory for the Europe that went further reforming itself for the new world challenges with a new treaty founding the European Union. The main reform was balancing the structural core of the Union giving prominence to Federalism, but by no means supremacy over the other two main theories of integration. The European Parliament became an important political actor in the internal decision-making sharing responsibility with the European Commission (Neofunctionalism) and the Council. (Intergovernmentalism) The balance of power of these three institutions was based on the co-decision system, currently ordinary system, where the European Commission propose the legislation and the Council and the EP amend and approve them after reaching a common agreement (Ellwood, 2014).

The increasing power of the Federalism was translated in a higher internal cohesion of the members of the Union and solved many issues related with the national sovereignty sharing it to improve the internal working system of the Union. Nevertheless the absence of deep reforms in the external policies of the Union was still under the control of the national governments of the member states, Intergovernmentalism to reach common agreements among the member states in external situations. Still the national sovereignty and the external national interest were more important that a common approach in the international arena. The absence of external conflict near the borders of the Union or the non-existence of any close threat disguised this lack of external power of the Union.

THE WAR IN YUGOSLAVIA

The former Republic of Yugoslavia was a multinational state located in the European region of the Balkans. The end of the Cold War and the collapse of authoritarian communist regimes meant at first some political instability translated into breakaway territories in Europe, as Estonia, Latvia and Lithuania, or simple disintegration of previous states as Czechoslovakia separated in two different states. The process was mostly done in peace with no major conflicts, but the case of Yugoslavia was to be different. The country was formed by four major nationalities, Serbians, Croatians, Bosnians and Slovenians, among other national minorities as Albanians or Hungarians. The process dismembering the state was very conflictive and led to a savage war (Kitayama, 2009).

The European Union, apparently a rising world power, was divided internally with different national interests and positions regarding Yugoslavia. In order to respect all the national interest the EU had its hands tied throughout the conflict, showing a great incapacity to stop the war in a neighbour territory located in the area of influence of the Union. Finally US intervened in the conflict and solved it manu militari.

The war in Yugoslavia showed the problems of the EU facing violent conflicts. Clearly the Union was a great success internally, but in Foreign Affairs was incapable influencing the external event, securing it's on border areas. As a way to solve this situation and use the great potential of the union in the international arena the Common Foreign and Security Policy was formulated and finally incorporated to the EU by the Treaty of Maastricht and recently reformed by the Treaty of Lisbon. The CFSP was built under Intergovernmentalism keeping intact the sovereignty of the member states basing the external actions on cooperation under the institutional framework of the union rather than integration.

The Enlargement to Central and East Europe

After the concerns rose by the Yugoslavian War over the international incapacity of the Union, the path of success came back through the expansion of the organization. The absence of international rivals or any other main obstacle was translated into the incorporation of 10 states to the union in a first wave and 2 more countries afterwards. This enlargement to Estonia, Latvia, Lithuania, Poland, Czech Republic, Slovakia, Hungary, Slovenia, Malta, Cyprus, Bulgaria and Romania increased enormously the territory and population of the Union also increasing its potential capacity for external action. It also increased the size of the European market and positively influenced the economic development of the new members.

The main original targets of the Union were once more successfully fulfilled; peace among its members and social stability through economic development. Nevertheless most of these countries also joined NATO for security reasons in order to be protected from any external threat, showing clearly the concerns of these countries about the capacity of the Union to protect its members in case of a violent conflict (Matković, 2004).

The Idea of Europe Ruling the XXI Century

The expansion of the European organization plus its economic performance in a growing connected world led to an optimistic and unrealistic vision about Europe in the foreign affairs. The main ideas behind the assumption of the EU leading the world affairs were two; the empire of Law and the international importance of the European Market.

The first idea was link with the globalization of the world affairs because the end of the Cold War had meant the abolition of the borders between the different ideological blocs. Also the incorporation of China to the world economy helped to create the idea of a common interest in the whole world. The EU as the leading international force in terms of integration had a vast expertise in making common rules for its members. Hence the most logical step was having adopted the European legislation and standards all over the world (Dwan, 2001).

The second issue, the European Market, was also link with the globalization process. The Common European Market with common rules was the most important market of the world in economic terms with links with all the other main economies of the world, as US, China, India or Russia, influencing trade and economic international relations. The presumption was clear; if you want to trade with the EU you will have to follow the European rules of the Common Market. The best example could be the merge between Honeywell and General Electric, two major American companies. The first was listed as 77th in the Fortune 500 America's ranking. Honeywell has a global workforce of approximately 130,000, of whom approximately 58,000 are employed in the United States. The company is headquartered in Morristown, New Jersey. On the other hand General Electric is listed the fourth-largest in the world among the Forbes Global 2000, a huge corporation with presence in most of the planet but also with headquarters in US.

General Electric announced in 2000 it would attempt to acquire Honeywell; at the time, Honeywell was valued at over $21 billion. The merger was cleared by American Anti-Trust authorities but was blocked by the European Commission's competition commissioner, Mario Monti, on July 3, 2001. This decision was taken on the grounds that GE's dominance of the large jet engine market (led by the General Electric CF34 turbofan engine), leasing services (GECAS), and Honeywell's portfolio of regional jet engines and avionics. Hence, two American companies obtained the permission of their native authorities but the prohibition of the European institutions; the deal was broken because the resulting company could not afford to lose access to the European market.

This was the soft power of the European Union: If anybody in the world wanted to deal with Europe, they had to follow the European rules, and these rules were made by the European alone. Of course this approach is just valid accepting the premise of a rational behaviour from the other part, a position leading to the most profitable situation for both parts. It is clearly a similar thought than Intergovernmentalism but without the basic precept of sharing major common values among the different parts in order to increase the predictability of all the partners (Moravcsik, 2000).

Finally the empire of Law was also for some years dominated by Europe by the concept of Universal jurisdiction, where local justice authorities, mainly European, could trial citizens of other states for crimes committed in other states. Crime could be prosecuted without any judicial link with the judicial system prosecuting the suspects (Kerikmäe, 2014). The worldwide expansion of the values of Human Rights made subject all the world citizens of the Empire of Law directed by Europe. Nevertheless, the European states are abandoning the concept of Universal Justice because of its international consequences, as most of the states of the world do not follow the European standards in terms of human rights. The clearest example is Spain, leading force in this topic, as the judge Baltasar Garzon accused the former dictator of Chile, Pinochet, of different charges against human rights. It became a milestone in the process and even the own judge years after was dismissed from the Spanish judicial career for his ambition of expanding his prerogatives to trial world citizens to the absolute limits. Afterwards numerous Spanish tribunals started actions against the authorities of different world states, as China for their crimes against humanity. Therefore the Spanish government in order to satisfy an important trade partner, the economic cost of financing lost court cases in the world and its own inability to implement court rulings, has changed the legislation abolishing the Universal jurisdiction. The Spanish governmental actions are being followed gradually by the rest of Europe, in another failure of the European Soft power in the Foreign Affairs (Farrell, 2005).

European Military Action in Libya

The world financial crisis staggered the foundations of the own existence of the European Union because its problems inside of the Euro group. Hence the international imagine of Europe was highly damaged and need and important restoration.

The Arab spring was seen as an example of the soft dominance of Europe all over the world. The European society and democracy was again an example to the rest of the world and an item to imitate, as Tunis or Egypt showed. Nevertheless the violent response of Gadafi in Libya and he's repression to the civil population triggered a military operation led by France and UK under the coordination of the US. The mission based on airstrikes was successful as Gadafi lost the civil confrontation and his life. The military action counted with the support of almost all the members of the EU and NATO. Many European states contributed to the war effort under the Franco-British intergovernmental cooperation, being a major European triumph in the international arena.

Soon after the war was ended the chaotic situation of Libya, the collapse of the Egyptian democracy and the long Syrian civil war have transformed the previous sensation of success into a great deception, increasing the incapacity of the EU in the external action.

There have been other military operations of France in Africa as for example Chad, Central African Republic or Ivory Coast under the traditional French Foreign Policy focus on Africa, but none of the rest of the members of the European Union has played a significant role in these actions as UK played in Libya. Hence these interventions of France are a consequence of centuries of the traditional involvement of France in African affairs and under no perception a European action. It is clearly national sovereignty over any European communal interest, national centralization versus cooperation (Conceição, 2014).

Conclusion

The main conclusions of the research included in this paper must be understood from an international perspective, from a view of an active player in the international arena, a player willing to participate and beneficiate actively of the international situation. Five conclusions can be drawn herein shall:

1. The EU is very successful in internal matters
2. The EU is a peace system, so obviously in the case of a no peaceful situation cannot succeed
3. The EU is working through Neofunctionalism and Intergovernmentalism, two paths that work well internally, but externally are extremely weak as they depend on rational behaviour of all the partners involved in a conflict. Federalism does not have any external influence in the European Union rather than vocational trips of the members of the European Parliament (Monar, 2015).
4. The expansion of the EU was its main tool for international influence. Currently with the borders defined in North, West and South by geographical borders, just East stands open for Europe. But as the enlargements are reaching the area of influence of Russia, the European Union is facing for the first time since the Cold War with a paramount obstacle and it's not ready to cope it.
5. Model changing: The European working systems includes after each reform more federal aspects, but still is far from being a federal state with a strong single voice abroad able to defend the European interest internationally against violent international actors. The members of the EU are facing currently a crucial decision for their citizens with two main options:
   a) No international interventions: The EU can work on basis of cooperation. It is a good internal system complemented with Neofunctionalism and Federalism, because it keeps the

national sovereignty if not intact at least with a high level of autonomy.

b) The EU as an international force: If the EU wants to act effectively in the international arena it has to sacrifice the national sovereignty in earnest of a common good. Cooperation and Neofunctionalism have proved good in internal matters but ineffective in foreign affairs, hence federalism should be the most likely path to international success.

REFERENCES

Börzel, T. A., & van Hüllen, V. (2014). One voice, one message, but conflicting goals: cohesiveness and consistency in the European Neighbourhood Policy. *Journal of European Public Policy*, *21*(7), 1033-1049.

Braudel, F. (1995). *A history of civilizations* (p. xi). Harmondsworth: Penguin books.

da Conceição-Heldt, E., & Meunier, S. (2014). Speaking with a single voice: internal cohesiveness and external effectiveness of the EU in global governance. *Journal of European public policy*, *21*(7), 961-979.

Dutt, P. K., & Kerikmäe, T. (2014). Concepts and Problems Associated with eDemocracy. In *Regulating eTechnologies in the European Union* (pp. 285-324). Springer International Publishing.

Dwan, R. (2001). Jean Monnet and the European Defence Community, 1950-54. *Cold War History*, 1(3), 141-160.

Ellingsen, T. (2000). Colorful community or ethnic witches' brew? Multiethnicity and domestic conflict during and after the Cold War. *Journal of Conflict Resolution*, 44(2), 228-249.

Ellwood, D. W. (2014). *Rebuilding Europe: Western Europe, America and Postwar Reconstruction*. Routledge.

Farrell, M. (2005). Editorial: EU External Relations: Exporting the EU Model of Governance? *European Foreign Affairs Review*, *10*(4), 451-462.

Hadfield, A., & Fiott, D. (2014). Relations with the Rest of the World: From Chaos to Consolidation? *JCMS: Journal of Common Market Studies*, *52*(S1), 170-185.

Hooghe, L., & Marks, G. (2009). A postfunctionalist theory of European integration: From permissive consensus to constraining dissensus. *British Journal of Political Science*, 39(01), 1-23.

Horga, I., & Dogot, C. M. (2012). Enlargement Process, Classic Geopolitics, and EU Internal Priorities. *Eurolimes*, (14), 161-184.

Howorth, J. (2004). Discourse, ideas, and epistemic communities in European security and defence policy. *West European Politics*, 27(2), 211-234.

Kerikmäe, T. (2014). EU Law and the Development of a Sustainable, Competitive and Secure Energy Policy. Opportunities and Shortcomings, by Bram Delvaux. (Antwerp: Intersentia, 2013). *Common Market Law Review*, *51*(3), 1044-1045.

Kitayama, S., Park, H., Sevincer, A. T., Karasawa, M., & Uskul, A. K. (2009). A cultural task analysis of implicit independence: comparing North America, Western Europe, and East Asia. *Journal of personality and social psychology*, 97(2), 236.

Lavenex, S. (2004). EU external governance in'wider Europe.' *Journal of European public policy*, *11*(4), 680-700.

Matković, V., Kostial, K., Simonović, I., Buzina, R., Brodarec, A., & Nordin, B. E. E. (1979). Bone status and fracture rates in two regions of Yugoslavia. *The American journal of clinical nutrition*, *32*(3), 540-549.

Mearsheimer, J. J. (1990). Back to the future: instability in Europe after the Cold War. *International security*, 5-56.

Menon, A., Forster, A., & Wallace, W. (1992). A common European defence?. *Survival,* 34(3), 98-118.

Monar, J. (2015). The EU as an International Counter-terrorism Actor: Progress and Constraints. *Intelligence and National Security*, (ahead-of-print), 1-24.

Moravcsik, A. (2000). De Gaulle between Grain and Grandeur: The Political Economy of French EC Policy, 1958–1970 (Part 2). *Journal of Cold War Studies*, 2(3), 4-68.

Murdoch, Z., Trondal, J., & GÄNZLE, S. (2014). Building foreign affairs capacity in the EU: The recruitment of member state officials to the European External Action Service (EEAS). *Public Administration*, *92*(1), 71-86.

Nye, J. S. (1970). Comparing common markets: a revised neo-functionalist model. *International Organization*, 24(04), 796-835.

Nyman-Metcalf, K., Dutt, P. K., & Chochia, A. (2014). The Freedom to Conduct Business and the Right to Property: The EU Technology Transfer Block Exemption Regulation and the Relationship between Intellectual Property and Competition Law. In *Protecting Human Rights in the EU* (pp. 37-70). Springer Berlin Heidelberg.

Pierson, P. (1996). The Path to European Integration A Historical Institutionalist Analysis. *Comparative political studies*, 29(2), 123-163.

Risse-Kappen, T. (1994). Ideas do not float freely: transnational coalitions, domestic structures, and the end of the cold war. *International Organization*, 48(02), 185-214.

Scott, A. J. (1988). Flexible production systems and regional development: the rise of new industrial spaces in North America and Western Europe*. *International Journal of Urban and Regional Research*, 12(2), 171-186.

Sweet, A. S., & Sandholtz, W. (1997). European integration and supranational governance. *Journal of European public policy*, 4(3), 297-317.

Troitiño, D. R. (2014). The British Position towards European Integration: A Different Economic and Political Approach. *Baltic Journal of European Studies*, 4(1), 119-136.

Wallace, W., & Smith, J. (1995). Democracy or technocracy? European integration and the problem of popular consent. *West European Politics*, 18(3), 137-157.

Waltz, K. N. (2000). Structural realism after the Cold War. *International security*, 25(1), 5-41.

Weller, M. (1992). The international response to the dissolution of the Socialist Federal Republic of Yugoslavia. *American Journal of International Law*, 569-607.

Wessel, R. A. (2000). The inside looking out: consistency and delimitation in EU external relations. *Common Market Law Review*, *37*(5), 1135-1171.

Wunsch, H., Angus, D. C., Harrison, D. A., Collange, O., Fowler, R., Hoste, E. A. ... & Rowan, K. M. (2008). Variation in critical care services across North America and Western Europe. *Critical care medicine*, 36(10), 2787-e8.

In: European Union
Editor: Wilbert Strickland

ISBN: 978-1-53612-359-3

Chapter 3

ONLINE PIRACY AND HUMAN RIGHTS: REFLECTIONS ON THE EUROPEAN APPROACH

Anna G. Micara[*]
Department of International, Legal, Historical and Political Studies,
University of Milan, Milan, Italy

ABSTRACT

Online piracy is a widespread and worrisome phenomenon that affects the intellectual property holders' rights and that could have detrimental effects for the economy of a country. On the other hand, the enforcement of intellectual property rights may affect human rights such as freedom of expression or the right to protection of personal data. This article analyzes the case-law of the EU on measures to fight online piracy so as to shed light on whether the Court of Justice of the European Union struck a fair balance between intellectual property and human rights. Also, the case-law of the European Court of Human Rights will be examined. It will be shown that the reasoning based on the balancing fundamental rights did not lead to greater legitimacy of intellectual

[*] Corresponding author: Email: annagiuliam@gmail.com.

property yet and that, from a more general perspective, the EU is shaping a *sui generis* regime compared to international law. The need for more guidance at the EU and international level strongly emerges.

Keywords: intellectual property rights, online piracy, freedom of expression, freedom to conduct business, right to personal data

1. Introduction

Intellectual property rights (IPRs) are commonly defined as incentives to innovation: authors and inventors enjoy an exclusive right as a reward in the short term until their work or invention goes to the public domain.[1] Therefore, they are crucial elements of the knowledge economy of several industrialized countries. Whereas piracy, i.e., infringement of copyright, and counterfeiting, i.e., infringement of industrial property rights (which include patent and trademarks) are worrisome phenomena having deep detrimental consequences for the industries' competitiveness and, in case of certain sensitive products such as medicines, for the health and safety of consumers.[2] Piracy and counterfeiting on the internet are widespread and growing as shows, for example, the fact that '[w]orldwide, 432.0 m unique internet users explicitly sought infringing content during January 2013'.[3] If, on the one hand, internet allows creators and inventors to exploit new ways to commercialise their works, on the other hand it makes much easier to get and to sell pirated and counterfeit goods: reference can be made to websites offering the possibility to share files, usually copyrighted music, such as peer to peer (P2P) networks and video streaming websites.

Online piracy has a deep relationship with human rights. First, measures of enforcement of IPRs may affect freedom of expression and

---

[1] See, among others, C Waelde, A Brown, S Kheria, J Cornwell (2016).

[2] On economic and social consequences of counterfeiting see, among others, M Schneider, O Vrins (2012), at 9-25.

[3] Netnames, *Sizing the piracy universe*, 2013, http://www.netnames.com/UserFiles/netnames-sizing_piracy_universe-report-2_5.pdf 3. For data on this phenomenon see also OECD, *Piracy of Digital Content*, July 2009 http://www.oecd.org/industry/ind/ piracy of digitalcontent.htm.

other human rights. At the international level, this clearly emerged and was intensely debated during the negotiations of the Anti-Counterfeiting Trade Agreement (ACTA),[4] an agreement that would have provided for civil, criminal and customs measures of enforcement as well as specific enforcement measures for the digital environment. The digital chapter (art. 27) was one of the most controversial issues: the last version mentioned that relevant fundamental rights such as freedom of expression and privacy should have been preserved but still measures to ensure their effective protection were lacking.[5] Before that, the inclusion of the so-called 'three strike test', i.e., the possibility of requiring cut off of internet access to users that committed online piracy (similar to the French HADOPI and the British Digital Economy Act[6]), was at issue but it was criticized by many, such as the Special Rapporteur to Freedom of Expression[7] and the European Data Protection Supervisor[8] and in the end it was withdrawn. However, ACTA raised a big movement of the civil society and, within the European Union (EU), it was rejected by the European Parliament.[9]

On the other hand, piracy affects the holders' property rights. In this regard, certain provisions of the Universal Declaration of Human Rights (UDHR), such as the 'right to own property' (art. 17) and 'the right to the protection of the moral and material interests resulting from any scientific,

---

[4] See ACTA text in Proposal for a Council Decision on the Conclusion of the Anti-Counterfeiting Trade Agreement Between the European Union and Its Member States, Australia, Canada, Japan, the Republic of Korea, the United Mexican States, the Kingdom of Morocco, New Zealand, the Republic of Singapore, the Swiss Confederation and the United States of America, 24 June 2011, COM(2011)380.

[5] See Opinion of European Academics on Anti-Counterfeiting Trade Agreement, http:// www. iri.uni-hannover.de/ tl_files/ pdf/ ACTA_opinion_110211_DH2.pdf, 6. See also R Matulionyte (2011) 252ff.

[6] C Geiger, (2011), 465ff; KK Garstka, (2012), 161ff. HADOPI was finally declared unconstitutional.

[7] Report of the Special Rapporteur on the promotion and protection of the right to freedom of opinion and expression (16 May 2011) UN Doc A/HRC/17/27, paras 49-50.

[8] Opinion of the European Data Protection Supervisor on the current negotiations by the European Union of an Anti-Counterfeiting Trade Agreement (ACTA), OJ 2010 C 147/1, paras 32ff.

[9] European Parliament legislative resolution of 4 July 2012 on the draft Council decision on the conclusion of the Anti-Counterfeiting Trade Agreement between the European Union and its Member States, Australia, Canada, Japan, the Republic of Korea, the United Mexican States, the Kingdom of Morocco, New Zealand, the Republic of Singapore, the Swiss Confederation and the United States of America (12195/2011 – C7-0027/2012 – 2011/0167(NLE)).

literary or artistic production of which he is the author' (art. 27.2),[10] which has been followed by the analogous art. 15.c of the International Covenant on Economic, Social and Cultural Rights (ICESCR), can be interpreted as protecting IPRs. However, after the enhancement of IPRs protection at the international level, mainly through the conclusion of the Trade-related Intellectual Property Rights (TRIPs) Agreement,[11] the extension of IPRs and their relationship with human rights was much debated, mainly over whether they are human rights (according to some authors they should have been considered 'privileges' rather than 'rights'[12]) and over whether human rights should prevail on them.[13] In this framework, the Committee on Economic, Social and Cultural Rights clarified that human rights and IPRs have different features: in particular, '[h]uman rights are fundamental, inalienable and universal entitlements belonging to individuals and … are fundamental as they are inherent to the human person as such'[14] whereas 'intellectual property rights are generally of a temporary nature, and can be revoked, licensed or assigned to someone else'.[15] Therefore,

> the scope of protection of the moral and material interests of the author provided for by article 15, paragraph 1 (c) [ICESCR], *does not* necessarily coincide with what is referred to as intellectual property rights under national legislation or international agreements (emphasis added).[16]

---

[10] On the negotiating history of this article see P. Yu, (2007), 1047-58.

[11] Trade-Related Aspects of Intellectual Property Rights Agreement, Annex 1C of the Agreement establishing the World Trade Organization (adopted 15 April 1994, entered into force 1 January 1995) 1869 UNTS 299.

[12] On this see, among others, HM Haugen (2005) 446ff; P Drahos (1998) 32.

[13] See, among others, T Mylly, (2005) 197; J Cornides, (2004) 135; AR Chapman, (2002) 861; UN High Commissioner for human rights, Sub-Commission on Human Rights, Resolution 2001/21, *Intellectual property and human rights*, UN Doc E.CN.4.SUB.2.RES.2001.21.En, para 3.

[14] Committee On Economic, Social and Cultural rights, General Comment No. 17, The right of everyone to benefit from the protection of the moral and material interests resulting from any scientific, literary or artistic production of which he or she is the author (article 15, paragraph 1 (c), of the Covenant) (12 January 2006) UN Doc E/C.12/GC/1712, para 1.

[15] Ibid. para 2.

[16] Ibid.

The debate on the relationship between intellectual property, and especially the measures for their enforcement, and human rights is not over but it still very lively and relevant case-law is growing.[17] Against this background, the article aims at analyzing the EU approach which is peculiar because, as will be shown, the growing case law of the Court of Justice of the European Union (CJEU) on IPRs enforcement, especially on online piracy, is featured by a fundamental rights' reasoning, usually aimed at balancing intellectual property, freedom to conduct business, freedom of expression and protection of personal data. This analysis will shed light on whether the CJEU is shaping a fair balance between IPRs and human rights and on broader implications from the human rights perspective.

2. The European Union Action against Piracy: The Need of a Renewed Consensus and the Role of Fundamental Rights

Although many aspects concerning enforcement of IPRs are still matter of national law, the EU undertook several actions in the framework of the realization of the internal market and of the common commercial policy and, nowadays, the need of an EU approach is more compelling due to the importance to shape the single digital market.[18]

Only in 1998 the Commission presented a Green Paper on counterfeiting and piracy[19] and then adopted Directive 2004/48 on the enforcement of IPRs, which aimed at ensuring effective means of enforcing those rights in order to encourage innovation and creativity and

[17] See, among others, C Geiger (2015); L Helfer, GW Austin (2011); W Grosheide (ed.) (2010); P Torremans (ed.) (2008). See also Report of the Special Rapporteur in the field of cultural rights Farida Shaheed, Copyright policy and the right to science and culture (24 December 2014) UN Doc A/HRC/28/57, paras 26-29 and 52-54.

[18] See Communication from the Commission to the European Parliament, the Council, the European Economic and Social Committee and the Committee of the Regions, *A Digital Single Market Strategy for Europe*, (6 May 2015) COM(2015)192.

[19] European Commission, Green Paper, Combating Counterfeiting and Piracy in the Single Market (15 October 1998) COM(98)569. Previously see Regulation 3842/86 laying down measures to prohibit the release for free circulation of counterfeit goods, [1986] *OJ* L 357/1.

for the proper functioning of the internal market.[20] The Directive harmonizes precautionary measures such as interlocutory injunctions and seizures, as well as corrective measures, such as permanent injunctions, recall, definitive removal from the channels of commerce, or destruction of the infringing goods. Whereas, injunctions related to copyright infringements are covered by the Information Society Directive[21] which provides that Member States 'shall ensure that right holders are in a position to apply for an injunction against intermediaries whose services are used by a third party to infringe a copyright or related right' (art. 8.3). Furthermore, the Electronic Commerce Directive (ECD)[22] harmonised some liability's exemptions of the Internet Service Providers (ISPs), in the event ISPs act as mere conduits (art. 12), caches (art. 13) or hosts of information (art. 14), and prevents general monitoring obligations (art. 15).

In the second half of 2000s the EU action became more intense but also more controversial. At the internal level, the European Observatory on Counterfeiting and Piracy was launched; the Commission submitted a proposal to harmonize criminal measures aimed at enforcing IPRs,[23] which was criticized[24] and then withdrawn in 2010; an attempt to include in the 'Telecom Package' the so-called graduated response measures (similar to the mentioned French measures providing for cutting internet to internet users infringing copyright[25]) has been unsuccessful.[26] At the external level,

[20] Directive 2004/48/EC on the enforcement of intellectual property rights [2004] OJ L 157/45.

[21] Directive 2001/29 on the harmonisation of certain aspects of copyright and related rights in the digital information society [2001] OJ L 167.

[22] Directive 2000/31/EC on certain legal aspects of information society services, in particular electronic commerce, in the Internal Market [2000] OJ L178/1.

[23] See the Proposal for a European Parliament and Council Directive on criminal measures aimed at ensuring the enforcement of intellectual property rights, COM(2005)276.

[24] See, among others, R Hilty, A Kur and A Peukert, (2006) 970. See also UNGA, Promotion and protection of the right to freedom of opinion and expression (10 August 2011) UN Doc A/66/290, para 40: according to the Special Rapporteur, given the importance of freedom of expression as a foundation of a democratic society, criminalization should be circumscribed to cases of child pornography, direct and public incitement to commit genocide, advocacy of national, racial or religious hatred that constitutes incitement to discrimination, hostility or violence, incitement to terrorism whereas other types of expression should not be criminalized 'as criminalization can be counter effective and the threat of harsh sanctions exert a significant chilling effect on the right to freedom of expression'.

[25] See n 6.

[26] See M Horten (2012). See also the final version of Directive 2009/140/EC amending Directives 2002/21/EC on a common regulatory framework for electronic communications

the EU was among the negotiators of the ACTA,[27] which, as mentioned, was rejected by the European Parliament, and, given the impossibility to achieve results at multilateral level, the EU started including enforcement provisions in its bilateral trade agreements.[28] And those issues even contributed to the creation of the Pirate Party, a political party first born in Sweden in 2006 (home of the famous website The Pirate Bay) which is represented at the European Parliament since 2014.[29]

Overall, the consequent need of enhancing social acceptance and legitimacy of IPRs in order to guarantee its enforcement[30] led the Commission to issue a Communication according to which '[t]he objective should be to arrive at a *renewed consensus* on how Intellectual Property Rights are exercised, and in a manner which fully involves all relevant stakeholders' (emphasis added)[31] and there has been a setback in advancing legislation so that several issues have been dealt with by the CJEU.

In this framework, the debate on the legitimacy of IPRs became deeply related to the one on the significance and interpretation of the new art. 17.2 of the EU Charter of Fundamental Rights (EUCFR)[32] according to which '[i]ntellectual property shall be protected'. Before the Charter, the right to property was protected in the EU legal order as a general principle of law.[33] In the 90s, when IPRs became crucial for the knowledge economies, it became clear that intellectual property had to be included in the notion of the fundamental right to property: in fact, the European Commission on Human Rights (predecessor of the European Court of Human Rights

networks and services, 2002/19/EC on access to, and interconnection of, electronic communications networks and associated facilities, and 2002/20/EC on the authorisation of electronic communications networks and services [2009] OJ L337/37, art. 1.3.a.

[27] See n 4.

[28] See, for example, Free Trade Agreement between the European Union and its Member States, of the one part, and the Republic of Korea, of the other part, [2011] *OJ* L 127/6, art. 10.41ff.

[29] See https://juliareda.eu.

[30] In this regard see also A Peukert, (2012), 151ff and Tyler (1997) 229.

[31] Communication from the Commission to the European Parliament, the Council and the European Economic and Social Committee, *Towards a renewed consensus on the enforcement of Intellectual Property Rights: An EU Action Plan* (1 July 2014) COM(2014)392/2, 4.

[32] Charter of Fundamental Rights of the European Union [2012] OJ C 326/391.

[33] 44/79, *Liselotte Hauer v Land Rheinland-Pfalz*, [1979] ECR 3727, para 17 and see, more in general, T Tridimas (2006) 301ff.

(ECtHR)) affirmed that patents fell within the notion of possession under art. 1 first protocol of the European Convention for the protection of human rights and fundamental freedoms (ECHR)[34] and the EUCFR, adopted in 2000, explicitly affirmed that IPRs are fundamental rights, acknowledging their 'growing importance'.[35] Since property was already protected, the explicit reassertion that IPRs are fundamental rights in the EUCFR led to an ongoing debate on the significance and on the contents of art. 17.2 which became related to the mentioned question of legitimacy of IPRs.[36] In fact, the human rights' nature of IPRs means that they are at the same level of other human rights and has effects on balancing them (Ubertazzi, 2007, p. 882). On the one hand, this, together with the fact that fundamental rights 'offer a synthesis of the bases of natural law and utilitarianism and represent the values from which intellectual property developed' (Geiger 2006 p. 382) could contribute to enhance the legitimacy of IPRs so that according to Geiger fundamental rights may be a 'new foundation for IP law' (Geiger 2006 p. 382). However, other authors claim that the human rights' nature of IPRs actually strengthens the rights of holders[37] and, from the perspective of human rights, several 'risks' have been identified such as 'lock-in', i.e., making difficult to change the case-law and existing secondary IPRs law (Mylly (2015) 127-28),[38] and the 'inflation of fundamental rights', meaning that 'the more things that are

---

[34] *Smith Kline and French laboratories Ltd. v the Netherlands*, Application No 12633/87, Commission Report, 4 October 1990, at 70. Afterwards, also the ECtHR affirmed that intellectual property is protected under art. 1 first protocol ECHR (see infra para 4). It is interesting to remind, though, that at the time of ECHR negotiation there was uncertainty on whether property should have been included so that it has been included in a protocol which is not ratified by all members i.e., Monaco and Switzerland have not ratified (on the elaboration of the first protocol of ECHR see, among others, CB Schutte, (2004) 16-22; AR Çoban, (2004) 127-137.

[35] *Text of the Explanations Relating to the Complete Text of the Charter*, CHARTE 4473/00, CONVENT 49, 11 October 2000, Explanation on Art. 17, 'Protection of intellectual property, one aspect of the right of property, is explicitly mentioned in paragraph 2 because of its growing importance and Community secondary legislation'.

[36] See, among others, A Peukert, (2015); P Torremans (2014) 502-17; J Griffiths, L McDonagh (2013); C Geiger, (2009) 113-17; L Ubertazzi, (2007) 881.

[37] J Janewa OseiTutu, (2015) 31ff. See also K Raustiala, (2007), 1031-32.

[38] .

claimed as being 'fundamental' or 'human' rights, the greater the risk that right language will become less persuasive'.[39]

Against this background, the analysis of the EU law on measures to enforce IPRs in the event of online piracy will shed light on this debate and will show that the fundamental rights balancing did not lead to greater IPRs legitimacy yet and, from a more general perspective, that the EU is shaping a *sui generis* regime compared to international law.

3. The Case-Law of the Court of Justice of the European Union and the Fair Balance of Fundamental Rights

Compared to piracy and counterfeiting offline, the fight against counterfeiting and piracy on the internet has specific features and need specific tools. In fact, when protected works are online they may be available for millions users so it is crucial to act quickly and preventively. This is why IPRs holders and collecting societies often demand preventive measures such as interlocutory injunctions. Furthermore, acting against real infringers, i. e. the internet user that uploads and shares a copyrighted work, could be really difficult so that in many cases IPRs holders act against intermediaries between internet contents and the users, the so-called ISPs such as Google, YouTube, or eBay. These are crucial actors since they have significant tools to stop infringements and they are easier to control compared to real infringers.

Another relevant feature, which is peculiar to the EU case-law on the enforcement of IPRs, is the need for a fair balance between IPRs and human rights. In *Promusicae*[40] the CJEU stated that

> Community law requires that, when transposing those directives, the Member States take care to rely on an interpretation of them which allows a *fair balance* to be struck between the various fundamental rights

[39] Griffiths, McDonagh (2013) 93; Mylly (2015) 129-30.

[40] C-275/06, *Productores de Música de España (Promusicae) v Telefónica de España SAU*, [2008] ECR I-271 paras 54 and 70.

> protected by the Community legal order. Further, when implementing the measures transposing those directives, the authorities and courts of the Member States must not only interpret their national law in a manner consistent with those directives but also make sure that they do not rely on an interpretation of them which would be in conflict with those fundamental rights or with the other general principles of Community law, such as the principle of *proportionality* (emphasis added).[41]

While in *Promusicae* the CJEU left the decision on the balance among fundamental rights to the national judge, in the following cases, analysed below, it furthered its reasoning, although national approaches still present divergences in some respects.

The rights mainly involved in this balance are intellectual property, freedom to conduct a business, freedom of information and the right to personal data.

As mentioned, the EUCFR only says that '[i]ntellectual property shall be protected' (art. 17.2) and there is an ongoing debate on the significance and contents of this article.[42] The Charter's explanation clarifies that art. 17.2 is based on art. 1 first protocol ECHR,[43] which refers to the social function of property, but there are still few cases to draw conclusions on whether this provision affects the exact extension and content of each IPR compared to previous case-law.[44] Furthermore, the CJEU reaffirmed that '[t]here is, … nothing whatsoever in the wording of that provision [art. 17.2 of the Charter] or in the Court's case-law to suggest that that right is inviolable and must for that reason be absolutely protected'[45] and therefore the proportionality principle becomes a crucial issue.

---

[41] Ibid., para 70.

[42] See n 36.

[43] *Text of the Explanations* (n 35). On art. 1 First Protocol ECHR see, among others, W Schabas (2015) 958-85.

[44] See for example C-547/14, *Philip Morris Brands SARL and Others v Secretary of State for Health*, 4 May 2016; C-477/14, *Pillbox 38 (UK) Ltd v The Secretary of State for Health*, 4 May 2016 and previous case C-491/01, *The Queen v Secretary of State for Health, ex parte British American Tobacco (Investments) Ltd and Imperial Tobacco Ltd* [2002] ECR I-11453. See also C-479/04, *Laserdisken ApS v Kulturministeriet*, [2006] ECR I-8089; C-347/03, *Regione autonoma Friuli-Venezia Giulia and Agenzia regionale per lo sviluppo rurale (ERSA) v Ministero delle Politiche Agricole e Forestali* [2005] ECR I-3785.

[45] C-70/10, *Scarlet Extended SA v Société belge des auteurs, compositeurs et éditeurs SCRL (SABAM)* [2011] ECR I-11959, para 43. See also previous case law 44/79, *Liselotte Hauer* (n 33) para 23.

Freedom to conduct business also has a vague formulation: art. 16 EUCFR says that '[t]he freedom to conduct a business in accordance with Union law and national laws and practices is recognized'. This right is based on the previous CJEU case-law on freedom to exercise an economic activity, freedom of contract and free competition.[46] Therefore, it is clear that it is not an absolute right and there is case-law but, as it is for intellectual property, it is still not clear if the inclusion in the Charter is affecting the significance and content of this freedom and there are still few cases on its application to ISPs.

Freedom of information is part of freedom of expression which, in fact, 'shall include freedom to hold opinions and to receive and impart information and ideas without interference by public authority and regardless of frontiers' (art. 11 of the Charter corresponding to art. 10 ECHR and to art. 19 UDHR).[47] Within the ECtHR case-law, internet broadened the scope of this freedom.[48]

Concerning protection of personal data, it has to be highlighted that the EUCFR introduced a specific right (art. 8) which is distinct from the 'right to respect for his or her private and family life, home and communications' (art. 7) i.e., the right to privacy, although they are strictly related (whereas within the ECHR personal data are protected within art. 8 on private and family life corresponding to art. 12 UDHR). Relevant case-law is growing as it is the EU competence in these matters, which also concerns privacy and electronic communications.[49]

Finally, the EUCFR provides for general exceptions to the protected fundamental rights according to which limitations must be provided for by law, respect the *essence* of those rights and freedoms and, under the principle of proportionality, they may be made to achieve EU general interest objectives or to protect rights and freedom of others (art. 52.1).

---

[46] *Text of the Explanations* (n 35), Explanation on Art. 16. See especially 4/74, *Nold*, ECR 491.

[47] See Woods, (2014) 311.

[48] W Benedek, MC Ketteman (2013) 27.

[49] Directive 2002/58/EC concerning the processing of personal data and the protection of privacy in the electronic communications sector [2002] OJ L 201. In general on the EU competence see GG Fuster, (2014) 111ff.

3.1. Filtering Systems in *Scarlet v SABAM*: A Fair Balance

In *Scarlet v Sabam*,[50] SABAM, a management company representing authors, composers and editors of musical works, brought interlocutory proceedings before the President of the Tribunal de première instance of Brussels against Scarlet, an ISP offering internet access, because users of Scarlet's services downloaded copyrighted material without SABAM's authorisation through P2P networks. Considering that Scarlet was the best placed to take relevant measures, SABAM sought and obtained an order requiring Scarlet to bring such infringements to an end 'by making it impossible for its customers to send or receive in any way files containing a musical work in SABAM's repertoire by means of peer-to-peer software, on pain of a periodic penalty'.[51] Scarlet appealed and the Court of Appeal asked the CJEU whether such an injunction was precluded by the Directives on Electronic Commerce,[52] Information society,[53] enforcement of IPRs[54], data protection[55] and privacy and electronic communications,[56] in the light of applicable fundamental rights.

The injunction at issue would have imposed to introduce

'a system for filtering

- all electronic communications passing via its [Scarlet] services, in particular those involving the use of peer-to-peer software
- which applies indiscriminately to all its customers;
- as a preventive measure;
- exclusively at its expense; and
- for an unlimited period,

[50] C-70/10, *Scarlet* (n 44).

[51] Ibid., para 23.

[52] Directive 2000/31/EC (n 22).

[53] Directive 2001/29/EC (n 21).

[54] Directive 2004/48/EC (n 20).

[55] Directive 95/46/EC of 24 October 1995 on the protection of individuals with regard to the processing of personal data and on the free movement of such data, [1995] OJ L 281.

[56] Directive 2002/58/EC (n 48).

- which is capable of identifying on that provider's network the movement of electronic files containing a musical, cinematographic or audio-visual work in respect of which the applicant claims to hold intellectual property rights, with a view to blocking the transfer of files the sharing of which infringes copyright'.[57]

According to the CJEU, such a filtering system would have required the ISP to actively monitor all communications transmitted on its network in order to determine lawful and unlawful files and, therefore, it was contrary to the prohibition of general monitoring provided for by the Electronic Commerce Directive (art. 15.1).[58]

However, the CJEU decided to judge also on whether the adoption of such an injunction would have struck a fair balance between applicable fundamental rights, according to *Promusicae* jurisprudence.[59] On the one hand, the filter aimed at ensuring protection of copyright, protected by art. 17.2 EUCFR. On the other hand, the ISP, i.e., Scarlet, would have 'to install a complicated, costly and permanent computer system at its own expense'[60] which amounted to a 'serious infringement' of its freedom to conduct business.[61] Therefore, the fair balance between protection of copyright and freedom to conduct a business was not struck.[62]

Furthermore, the CJEU made some considerations on the right to protection of personal data and the freedom to receive or impart information enjoyed by ISPs customers. In this regard, the filter

> could potentially undermine freedom of information since that system might not distinguish adequately between unlawful content and lawful content, with the result that its introduction could lead to the blocking of lawful communications.[63]

[57] C-70/10, *Scarlet* (n 44), para 29.
[58] Ibid., para 40.
[59] C-275/06, *Productores de Música* (n 39).
[60] Ibid., para 48.
[61] Ibid., para 48.
[62] Ibid., para 49.
[63] Ibid., para 52.

Also, the filter would have involved the collection and identification of users' Internet Protocol (IP) addresses, which are protected personal data,[64] from which unlawful content on the network is sent.

In conclusion, an injunction requiring such a filtering system would not have met the requirement that a fair balance was struck between the involved fundamental rights.[65]

Filtering systems are very useful and effective preventive tools to enforce IPRs against massive infringement. Overall, this judgment does not prohibit filters *per se* since it does not preclude filtering systems having different features. However, if limitation in time may be feasible, the feasibility in terms of the costs for ISPs, i.e., to install and maintain the filter, appears more problematic (and therefore a serious infringement of freedom to conduct business) unless technology will evolve. Moreover, shaping a filter consistent with right of information of the users, i.e., able to distinguish legal content, also appears difficult and more guidance is desirable: for example, according to the Recommendations of the Committee of Ministers of the Council of Europe, those systems should avoid unreasonable blocking content, provide for effective means of recourse (including suspension of filters) and avoid general blocking of content *ratione personae* (i.e., taking into account users that need access to content for research purpose).[66] Therefore, especially this last recommendation makes very difficult to have a 'legitimate' filtering system capable to identify different categories of users. Unfortunately, similar guidance on filters and data protection has not been elaborated so far.

---

[64] Ibid., para 51.

[65] Ibid. para 53.

[66] Recommendation of the Committee of Ministers to member States on measures to promote the respect for freedom of expression and information with regard to Internet filters CM/Rec(2008)6, 26 March 2008.

3.2. Online Blocking Injunction in *UPC Telekabel*: An Unfair Balance?

In *UPC Telekabel*[67] the injunction at issue consisted in the obligation for the ISP UPC Telekabel to block access of its customers to a website (kino.to) that made available films protected by copyright without consent of the film production companies Constantin Film and Wega. According to the Handelsgericht Wien (Commercial Court, Wien) UPC Telekabel should have blocked the domain name of the website and the IP. However, upon appeal, the Oberlandesgericht Wien held that the ISP could only be required an outcome injunction, aimed at achieving the result of preventing its customers the access to the website, whereas means to be used could have been decided by UPC Telekabel.

The CJEU had to verify if a fair balance was struck among intellectual property, freedom to conduct business and freedom of information. Concerning freedom to conduct a business, which ‘includes, inter alia, the right for any business to be able to freely use, within the limits of its liability for its own acts, the economic, technical and financial resources available to it’,[68] such an injunction would have restricted it due to its costs and impact on management of the ISP activities but it did not infringe the ‘very substance’[69] of it thanks to the flexibility the ISP had in implementing the injunction (as said, it was an outcome injunction) and because it allowed the ISP to avoid liability by proving to have taken all reasonable measures.[70]

Concerning freedom of information of internet users, the CJEU affirmed that

[67] C-314/12, *UPC Telekabel Wien GmbH v Constantin Film Verleih GmbH and Wega Filmproduktionsgesellschaft mbH*, ECLI:EU:C:2014:192.

[68] Ibid., para 49.

[69] Ibid., para 51.

[70] Ibid., paras 52-53.

> the measures adopted by the internet service provider must be strictly targeted, in the sense that they must serve to bring an end to a third party's infringement of copyright or of a related right but without thereby affecting internet users who are using the provider's services in order to lawfully access information.[71]

Furthermore, internet users must have the possibility to assert their rights before the Court once the ISP adopted its implementing measures.[72] Therefore, according to the CJEU, an online blocking injunction not imposing specific measures was not inconsistent with freedom of information *per se* but the national judge should have assessed that case-by-case.[73]

Concerning IPRs protection, the CJEU made some considerations on the effectiveness of the injunction, stating that it is possible that the enforcement of that injunction does not lead to a complete cessation of the infringements but measures taken by ISP when implementing the injunction must be sufficiently effective to ensure IPRs protection,[74] being able, at least, to make it difficult and seriously discourage internet users from accessing illegal contents (something to be assessed by national judges).[75] In this regard, after *UPC Telekabel*, kino.to was replaced by kinox.to. However, the question is at issue again before CJEU in a case concerning The Pirate Bay website where the defendant contest the (un)effectiveness of the online blocking.[76]

In conclusion, according to the CJEU a fair balance was struck.

Nonetheless, online blocking injunctions are particularly sensitive from the human rights perspective. General Comment n. 34 on freedom of expression explicitly referred to restrictions on the operation of website affirming that '[p]ermissible restrictions generally should be content-specific; generic bans on the operation of certain sites and systems are not

[71] Ibid., para 56.
[72] Ibid., para 57.
[73] Ibid., para 57.
[74] Ibid., para 63.
[75] Ibid., para 64.
[76] See Opinion of Advocate General Szpunar in Case C-610/15, *Stichting Brein v Ziggo BV, XS4ALL Internet BV*, ECLI:EU:C:2017:99.

compatible with paragraph 3'[77] [of art. 19 of the International Covenant on Civil and Political Rights (ICCPR)].[78] In fact, the ICCPR specifies that restrictions of freedom of expression and information must comply with the three-part cumulative test (art. 19.3), as reiterated by the 2014 *EU Human Rights Guidelines on Freedom of Expression Online and Offline*,[79] so that restrictions must be provided for by law, necessary to protect the rights of others (such as IPRs) and subject to the proportionality principle. Although the General Comment is clear on the inconsistency of generic bans on websites with art. 19.3 of the Covenant, it has to be noted that blocking access of a website sharing exclusively or predominantly illegal content may be deemed proportionate and even 'content-specific': one thing is to block access to the Pirate Bay, another is to block access to Youtube. The fact that films protected by copyright, such as in the case at issue, may be considered as political or artistic expression or expression with public aims does not prejudice the need to balance freedom of expression and information with copyright. However, also in this case more guidance is needed and, in this regard it is interesting to mention a concurrent opinion of judge Pinto de Albuquerque promoting the definition of minimum criteria for blocking measures consistent with ECHR (such as definition of categories of blocking orders i.e., blocking of entire websites or IP addresses, a limit on the duration of the blocking order, a definition of competent authorities to issue the order and a judicial appeal procedure).[80]

Also the ECtHR dealt with blocking injunctions in a case on a Turkish Court order to block the Google Sites domain. The block involved not only a website of a person accused of a crime but also the website that Mr Yildirim used to publish his academic works. The judgment is interesting

[77] Human Rights Committee, General Comment No. 34, Article 19: Freedoms of opinion and expression (12 September 2011), UN Doc CCPR/C/GC/34, para 43.

[78] International Covenant on Civil and Political Rights (adopted 16 December 1966, entered into force 23 March 1976), 999 UNTS 171.

[79] Council of the European Union, EU Human Rights Guidelines on Freedom of Expression Online and Offline, http:// eeas.europa.eu/delegations/documents/ eu_human_rights_guidelines_on_freedom_of_expression_online_and_offline_en.pdf, 12 May 2014, 18.

[80] *Ahmet Yildirim v. Turkey*, Application No 3111/10, Merits and Just Satisfaction, 18 December 2012, 27-28. More in general see also P Savola, (2014), 116.

because the Court stated that 'Article 10 does not prohibit prior restraints on publication as such'[81]: therefore preventive measures as blocking injunctions may be consistent with art. 10 ECHR but 'the dangers inherent in prior restraints are such that they call for the most careful scrutiny on the part of the Court'.[82]

The other crucial argument is whether outcome injunctions are consistent with human rights. The fact that the courts or administrative authorities do not specify the measures to be taken by the ISP raises doubts from several points of view. As underlined by the previous Special Rapporteur on freedom of expression, Frank La Rue, 'intermediaries, as private entities, are not best placed to make determination of whether a particular content is illegal, which require careful balancing of competing interests and consideration of defences'[83] whereas judicial authorities or other independent bodies should be competent to determine what content should be blocked to avoid censorship.[84] Moreover, ISPs can adopt the most restrictive measures from the freedom of expression perspective in order to avoid liability[85] and, therefore, 'censorship measures should *never* be delegated to a private entity, and that no one should be held liable for content on the Internet of which they are not the author'(emphasis added).[86] The merit of specifying implementing measures was also underlined by Advocate General Cruz Villalón.[87] In fact, there are several

[81] *Ahmet Yildirim* (n 79) para 47.

[82] Ibid., para 47. See also previous case *The Sunday Times v the United Kingdom* (No 2), Application No. 13166/87, Merits and Just Satisfaction, 26 November 1991, para 51.

[83] Report of the Special Rapporteur A/HRC/17/27 (n 7) para 42.

[84] UNGA, A/66/290 (n 26) para 38.

[85] Report of the Special Rapporteur A/HRC/17/27 (n 7), para 42. See also McNamee, 'The slide from "self-regulation" to corporate censorship, the scale and significance of moves to entrust internet intermediaries with a cornerstone of democracy – open electronic communication networks' (2011) https://edri.org/files/EDRI_selfreg_final_20110124.pdf.

[86] Ibid., para 43. See also, although on a different field, Opinion of the European Data Protection Supervisor of 10 May 2010 on the proposal for a directive of the European Parliament and of the Council on combating the sexual abuse, sexual exploitation of children and child pornography, repealing Framework Decision 2004/68/JHA, [2010] OJ C 323, para 11.

[87] Opinion of Advocate General Cruz Villalón in case C-314/12, *UPC Telekabel Wien GmbH v Constantin Film Verleih GmbH and Wega Filmproduktionsgesellschaft mbH*, ECLI:EU:C:2013:781, para 85.

ways to block a website that have different impacts on fundamental rights[88] and the Advocate General properly highlighted that a fair balance must be struck when the injunction is issued while according to the CJEU relevant considerations may be examined at a later stage.[89]

In this regard, it is interesting to mention again the case *Ahmet Yildirim v. Turkey*, because the ECtHR affirmed that the interference to art. 10 ECHR was not 'prescribed by law' since the Turkish Court made a decision referring to a recommendation from the competent administrative authority 'without ascertaining whether a less far-reaching measure could have been taken to block access specifically to the offending website'[90] and without weighing up various interests at stake i.e., without taking into account that blocking the Google Sites domain would have substantially restricted the rights of users.[91]

Taking into account the abovementioned considerations, the fact that the CJEU allowed an outcome injunction would lead to conclude that a fair balance was not struck. However, it is impossible to neglect that courts may not be able to address huge numbers of requests of copyright protection online. A similar problem raises with regard to notice and take down procedures (NTDs): of course in principle a court order better ensures respect for fundamental rights for the reasons mentioned above by the Special Rapporteur[92] but the reality is that NTDs are a fundamental tool and, as has been underlined, focus on official notifications would lead to *de facto* providers' exemption from liability because enforcement will often be too late and authorities do not have capacity and resources to pursue every infringement.[93]

[88] Ibid., para 86.
[89] Ibid. para 88. See also the considerations in M Husovec, M Peguera (2015).
[90] *Ahmet Yildirim* (n 79), para 64.
[91] Ibid., para 66.
[92] On the difficulties in assessing illegal materials see also P Van Eecke, (2011) 1465ff; Verbiest, Spindler, Riccio Van der Pierre, (2007), 14.
[93] Verbiest et al. (2007) 98.

3.3. Cutting Internet Access and Password-Protected Connections in *Mc Fadden v Sony*: A Fair Balance?

In *McFadden v Sony*[94] Mr Mc Fadden, a seller of lighting and sound systems, operated close to his business a wireless local area network (WLAN) free of charge whose access was anonymous, with the aim to attract customers of near-by shops or passers-by. By means of that WLAN a musical work, whose phonogram was produced by Sony, was made available to the general public on the internet without the consent of the IPRs holders so this led to proceedings on the direct and indirect liability of Mr McFadden for the use of the WLAN by a third party.

The Court of first instance dismissed Mr McFadden action. On appeal, the Landgericht München I decided to ask the CJEU how to interpret the Directives on Information Society,[95] on enforcement of IPRs,[96] and on Electronic Commerce (with regard to mere conduit's exemption)[97] and fundamental rights in order to assess whether relevant EU provisions would have precluded the measures considered by the national judge i.e., granting an injunction to the provider consisting in terminating or password-protecting the internet connection or in examining all communications passing through it.

Concerning the measure consisting in examining all communications passing through an internet connection, the CJEU stated that this was clearly contrary to art. 15.1 of the Electronic Commerce Directive which prevents EU member states from imposing a general obligation to monitor to providers.[98]

---

94 C-484/14, *Tobias McFadden v Sony Music Entertainment Germany Gmbh*, ECLI:EU:C:2016:689.

95 Directive 2001/29/EC (n 21).

96 Directive 2004/48/EC (n 20).

97 See Directive 2000/31/EC (n 22), art. 12.1 ECD: 'Where an Information Society service is provided that consists of the transmission in a communication network of information provided by a recipient of the service, or the provision of access to a communication network, Member States shall ensure that the service provider is not liable for the information transmitted, on condition that the provider: (a) does not initiate the transmission; (b) does not select the receiver of the transmission; and (c) does not select or modify the information contained in the transmission'.

98 C-484/14, *McFadden* (n 93) para 87.

Concerning the measure consisting in terminating the internet connection completely, the CJEU balanced intellectual property and freedom to conduct business and found that a fair balance was not struck[99] since such an injunction would have caused

> a serious infringement of the freedom to conduct a business of a person who pursues an economic activity, albeit of a secondary nature, consisting in providing internet access by categorically preventing that provider from pursuing the activity in practice in order to remedy a limited infringement of copyright without considering the adoption of measures less restrictive of that freedom.[100]

Finally, concerning the measure consisting in password-protecting an internet connection, the CJEU acknowledged that such an injunction was able to restrict freedom to conduct business but it would not have damaged the essence of it since it is 'limited to marginally adjusting one of the technical options open to the provider in exercising its activity"[101] (whereas according to the Advocate General it could have discouraged undertakings to offer that service[102]).

Similarly, password-protecting the connection would have restricted the right to freedom of information of the recipients of that service but it would not have undermined its essence since it was limited to requesting a password and was only one among several connections that can be used to access internet.[103] The Court also reiterated that the relevant injunction must be 'strictly targeted'[104] so as to be a proportional restriction to freedom of information whereas password-protecting the connection did not seem to be capable of restricting access to lawful information because it did not block any website.[105]

---

[99] Ibid. para 89.
[100] Ibid., para 88.
[101] Ibid., para 91.
[102] Opinion of Advocate General Spuznar in case C-484/14, *Tobias McFadden v Sony Music Entertainment Germany Gmbh*, ECLI:EU:C:2016:170, paras 138-39.
[103] Ibid., para 92.
[104] Ibid., para 93. See C-314/12, *UPC Telekabel* (n 66) para 56.
[105] Ibid., para 94.

Moreover, the injunction has been deemed as 'sufficiently effective'[106] to ensure intellectual property protection i.e., dissuading infringers that cannot act anonymously.[107] Effectiveness is a problem also in this case since those measures may easily be circumvented with false data[108] but, on the other hand, considering that effectiveness is a deep problem to fight digital piracy the need to allow some measures has to be taken into account.

In conclusion, only password-protecting the internet connection may be a measure capable of striking a fair balance among relevant fundamental rights. This judgment has been criticized, among others, by a group of industry players, claiming that this measure would stifle innovation and growth to which open WiFis contribute,[109] as well as by the Pirate Party which contested that "[f]ollowing its logic using public telephone booths and letterboxes should require identification, too"[110] and this would hinder free exchange of ideas and information on the internet. It is therefore desirable that the EU legislator will address those concerns.

3.4. The Right of Information of Directive 2004/48

Directive 2004/48 on IPRs enforcement provides a relevant tool for online piracy and counterfeiting: the so-called right of information according to which competent judicial authorities may order infringers or other persons offering commercial scale services used for the infringement to reveal information on the origin and distribution networks of the infringing goods or services (art. 8). This enables holders to identify infringers and alleged infringers and bring proceedings against them.

In the event of online piracy the right of information may be invoked to ask ISPs the IP address of internet users in order to identify infringers.

[106] Ibid., para 95. See also C-314/12, *UPC Telekabel* (n 66 para 62.

[107] Ibid., para 96.

[108] Opinion of Advocate General Spuznar in Case C-484/14 *McFadden* (n 101) para 146.

[109] Prohibiting Open WiFi is an Obstacle to Legitimate Trade https:// www.eff.org/ files/ 2015/ 07/20/closedwifiasanobstacletolegitimatetrade-4.pdf.

[110] *Top Court closes down open password-free WiFi in Europe*, 15 September 2016, http:// www. patrick-breyer.de/?p=561232.

The first relevant case before the CJEU dealt with an organization of producers and publishers of musical and audiovisual recordings (Promusicae) that asked the Spanish judge to order the ISP Telefónica to disclose the identities and physical addresses of certain persons whom it provided with internet access services and whose IP address and date and time of connection were known. These people allegedly shared copyrighted phonograms through the KaZaA file exchange program P2P and Promusicae intended to bring civil proceedings for copyright infringement. The CJEU affirmed that EU law did not require Member States to provide for an obligation to communicate personal data in the context of civil proceedings.[111]

Soon after the Court handled a similar case, concerning the request by certain publishing companies having exclusive rights on some audiobooks to the Swedish judge to order an ISP to disclose data in civil proceedings.[112] The CJEU stated that the Swedish legislation ensured a fair balance between IPRs protection enjoyed by copyright holders and the protection of personal data enjoyed by internet subscribers or users.[113] In fact, that legislation provided the right of information under certain conditions: in particular that

> there be clear evidence of an infringement of an intellectual property right, that the information can be regarded as facilitating the investigation into an infringement of copyright or impairment of such a right and that the reasons for the measure outweigh the nuisance or other harm which the measure may entail for the person affected by it or for some other conflicting interest.[114]

Thus, according to the Court, that legislation enabled the national courts 'to weigh the conflicting interests involved, on the basis of the facts of each case and taking due account of the requirements of the principle of proportionality'.[115]

---

[111] C-275/06, *Productores de Música* (n 40) paras 54 and 70.

[112] C-461/10, *Bonnier Audio AB, Earbooks AB, Norstedts Förlagsgrupp AB, Piratförlaget AB, Storyside AB v Perfect Communication Sweden AB*, ECLI:EU:C:2012:219.

[113] Ibid., para 60.

[114] Ibid., para. 58.

[115] Ibid., para. 59.

Although dealing with trademark infringement, it is also interesting the case *Coty Germany* where right of information prevailed over banking secrecy. In fact, the right of information is intended to implement the right to an effective remedy (art. 47 EUCFR) and indirectly IPRs (art. 17.2 EUCFR), and a legislation on banking secrecy which allows in an unlimited and unconditional manner to refuse information does not respect the essence of rights protected by the Charter as required by art. 52.1.[116]

The right of information is a relevant tool for IPRs holders. Similar provisions are present in the Regulation on custom enforcement of IPRs.[117] However, it has to be shaped in a way consistent with personal data protection. This means that the disclosure should be controlled by a judicial authority, that the processing of data on IPRs infringements by IPRs should be allowed only for the purpose of their litigation under specific conditions and the gravity of IPRs infringement has to be taken into account.[118] This is particularly relevant considering that there are still disparities among EU member states on the application of the right of information, which in some members is applied restrictively due to legislation on protection and retention of personal data.[119] However, effectiveness may again be a problem: even when disclosed, data could be false, different persons may use the same computer and certain infringers

---

116 C-580/13, *Coty Germany GmbH v Stadtparkasse Magdeburg*, ECLI:EU:C:2015:485, para 43.

117 Regulation 608/2013 of 12 June 2013 concerning customs enforcement of intellectual property rights and repealing Council Regulation (EC) No 1383/2003, [2013] OJ L 181, arts 17.4, 18.5 and 21 (see C-223/98, *Adidas AG*, [1999] ECR I-7081, paras 28-29). See also C-324/09, *L'Oréal SA and Others v eBay International AG and Others* [2011] ECR I-6011, para 142 on the possibility to order an operator of an online marketplace to take measures to identify its customer-sellers.

118 Opinion of the European Data Protection Supervisor on the proposal for a Council Decision on the Conclusion of the Anti-Counterfeiting Trade Agreement between the European Union and its Member States, Australia, Canada, Japan, the Republic of Korea, the United Mexican States, the Kingdom of Morocco, New Zealand, the Republic of Singapore, the Swiss Confederation and the United States of America https:// secure.edps.europa.eu/ EDPSWEB/webdav/shared/Documents/Consultation/Opinions/2012/12-04-24_ACTA_EN.pdf, paras 43-49.

119 Report from the Commission to the European Parliament, the Council, the European Economic and Social Committee and the Committee of the Regions, Application of Directive 2004/48/EC of the European Parliament and the Council of 29 April 2004 on the enforcement of intellectual property rights, COM(2010)779, 7.

may operate anonymously; moreover, requested data could not have been stored or already been erased.[120]

4. The Case Law of the European Court of Human Rights: A Cautious Approach

In order to better understand the CJEU case-law on online piracy it is important to refer to the relevant ECtHR case-law on these aspects due to the deep relationship between the CJEU case-law on fundamental rights and the ECtHR system, a relationship that is not possible to further here.[121]

As mentioned, the first cases on intellectual property date back the 90s and in 2007 the Grand Chamber of the ECtHR definitively clarified that intellectual property is protected under art. 1 of the first protocol ECHR.[122] However, relevant case-law is still scarce. The ECtHR interpreted the notion of possession rather broadly since even trademark applications are included in that notion[123] referring to the fact that, also before registration, applicants have proprietary rights and interests that may be licensed or sold and may have financial value. However, in the case at issue there was no interference with the peaceful enjoyment of that possession and therefore no violation of art. 1 first protocol ECHR so the extension of protection of trademark applications is still uncertain.[124] In another case, *Dima v. Romania*,[125] an artist, charged by a Parliamentary commission to create the design of a national emblem to be submitted to the Parliament, claimed that, being the author, Romanian authorities using the emblem should have paid him whereas the Supreme Court ruled that the State emblem could not be protected by copyright. However, the claim was held inadmissible.

[120] Commission, Synthesis of the responses "Civil enforcement of intellectual property rights: public consultation on the efficiency of proceedings and accessibility of measures", July 2013, 12-13.

[121] See, among others, V Kosta, N Skoutaris, V Tzevelekos (eds), *The EU accession to the ECHR* (Hart Publishing 2014).

[122] *Anheuser Busch Inc. v Portugal*, Application No 73049/01, Merits and Just Satisfaction, 11 January 2007, para 72.

[123] Ibid., para 78.

[124] For a comment see, among others, D Beiter, (2008) 715-17.

[125] *Dima c. Roumanie*, Application No 58472/00, decision, 26 May 2005.

Finally, in *Balan v Moldova*,[126] Moldavian authorities used a photograph as background for Moldovan identity cards without the consent of the author and without payment. A first proceeding ended with an award for compensation but, after the continued unlawful use of the photograph, a second legal action was dismissed because the court had not prohibited the future use of the photograph and the applicant did not request such a prohibition. The ECtHR concluded that there was interference with art. 1 first protocol ECHR, since "the illegal character of unauthorised use is not conditioned in the law by any particular act of the copyright owner",[127] which was not proportionate to the aim pursued since the public interest of issuing identity cards could have been reached without violating the right of the applicant.[128] Therefore, it is soon to draw conclusion on the case law of the ECtHR but it appears desirable, as Helfer underlined, that the Court adopt a 'rule of law' approach aimed at targeting arbitrary government conduct whereas it would be less justifiable an approach aimed at shaping intellectual property law in Europe (Helfer 2008, p. 51).[129]

There are also cases dealing specifically with IPRs enforcement measures that came at issue from the perspective of art. 10 ECHR on freedom of expression. ECtHR case-law on freedom of expression is broad and consolidated: the scope of application is very wide (it also applies to means of transmission[130]) and interferences should be prescribed by law, pursue a legitimate aim and necessary in a democratic society (art. 10.2 ECHR).[131]

In *Ashby Donald and others v France*,[132] pictures taken at fashion shows in Paris were published on a website in order to be sold without the

---

[126] *Balan v Moldova*, Application No 19247/03, Merits and Just Satisfaction, 29 January 2008.

[127] Ibid. para 38.

[128] Ibid. para 45.

[129] On the role of the ECtHR on intellectual property see also Griffiths, McDonagh (2013) 83-88.

[130] *Fredrik Neij and Peter Sunde Kolmisoppi against Sweden*, Application No 40397/12, decision, 19 February 2013.

[131] 'Freedom of expression constitutes one of the essential foundations of such a society, one of the basic conditions for its progress and for the development of every man' (*Handyside v United Kingdom* Application No 5493/72, 7 December 1976, para 49). See, among others, DJ Harris, M O'Boyle, C Warbrick, (2014) 613ff; Oetheimer (2012).

[132] *Ashby Donald and others v. France*, Application No 36769/08, Merits and Just Satisfaction, 10 January 2013.

authorisation of fashion houses holding copyright on the creations shown at the fashion shows. For the first time the ECtHR clarified that a conviction for copyright violation may constitute an interference to freedom of expression but recognized a very wide margin of appreciation to States in verifying whether the interference was necessary in a democratic society and concluded that there was no violation of art. 10 ECHR. In fact, the copyrighted material at issue was mainly a commercial expression not contributing to a debate of general interest[133] and national judges are better placed to assess the so-called 'pressing social need' capable of justifying interference with other protected rights.[134]

The following case *Neij and Sunde Kolmisoppi v Sweden*[135] concerned two people involved in the operation of the website 'The Pirate Bay', a known file sharing website, and convicted for copyright violation in Sweden. The ECtHR reminded that 'in the light of its accessibility and its capacity to store and communicate vast amounts of information, the Internet plays an important role in enhancing the public's access to news and facilitating the sharing and dissemination of information generally'[136] and, therefore, the website operated by the applicants was a mean to impart and receive information protected by art. 10 ECHR. Also in this case the conviction of the applicants was deemed an interference to freedom of expression but, again, the Court left a wide margin of appreciation, showing a cautious approach in balancing freedom of expression and the right to property. In fact, the enforcement measures were considered as proportionate since IPRs were seriously impaired, due to the nature of shared information and since 'the applicants had not taken any action to remove the torrent files in question, despite having been urged to do so'[137] even though damages amounted to 5 million euros.[138]

---

[133] On commercial expression see, among others, Harris, O'Boyle, Warbrick, (2014) 635-39.

[134] See *Case Of Chassagnou And Others v. France*, Applications Nos 25088/94, 28331/95 and 28443/95, Merits and Just Satisfaction, 29 April 1999, para 113.

[135] *Fredrik Neij* (n 129).

[136] Ibid., 9.

[137] Ibid., 11.

[138] In this regard it has to be mentioned that in *Ashby Donald* (n 131) the ECtHR would have considered whether the measured would have "financially strangled" the applicants but they did not show any evidence whereas in Neij the applicants did not rise this point.

Furthermore, although the ECHR does not include freedom to conduct business, the ECtHR took into account ISPs interests in two cases which take different conclusions so that it has to be seen which way forward the Court will take on these aspects.

Delfi AS v. Estonia[139] dealt with a news internet portal which published an article that was commented by several people. Around 20 comments contained language amounting to hate speech against a member of a company that asked to remove them. Delfi removed them immediately but refused the claim for damages. The Supreme Court stated that Delfi should have prevented unlawful comments from being published and failed to remove contents on its own initiative. The ECtHR had to assess whether the interference of freedom of expression was necessary in a democratic society in the interests of the protection of the reputation or rights of others and concluded that there was no violation of art. 10. This was confirmed by the Grand Chamber[140] whereas according to judges Sajó and Tsotsoria the judgment was 'an invitation to self-censorship at its worst'.[141]

In the following *MTE v. Hungary*[142], Magyar Tartalomszolgáltatók Egyesülete (MTE), a self-regulatory body of Hungarian internet providers whose tasks are monitoring the implementation of a professional code and operating an arbitration commission, published an article on unethical conduct of two real estate management websites. A user under pseudonym left an offensive comment so the company operating the concerned websites brought a civil action against MTE and the news portal Index.hu that had to pay damages. The ECtHR, also relying on the fact that the applicants had NTDs system and that filtering comments would require excessive forethought able to undermine freedom of information,[143] found a violation of art. 10 ECHR.

---

[139] *Delfi AS v. Estonia*, Application No 64569/09, Merits and Just Satisfaction, 10 October 2013.
[140] *Delfi AS v. Estonia*, Application No 64569/09, Merits and Just Satisfaction, 16 June 2015.
[141] Ibid., at 68.
[142] *Magyar Tartalomszolgáltatók Egyesülete and Index.hu Zrt v. Hungary*, Application No 22947/13, Merits and Just Satisfaction, 2 February 2016.
[143] Ibid., at 80-83.

Finally, although the ECtHR dealt extensively with privacy and data protection under art. 8 ECHR,[144] there are no cases on the balancing with IPRs in the digital environment yet.

5. What Impact on Legitimacy of Intellectual Property Rights Within the European Union?

A significant feature rising from the analyzed case-law is that the balance between the IPRs protection and freedom to conduct business appears predominant. In *Scarlet v SABAM* the filtering system did not struck a fair balance between fundamental rights mainly because it was deemed too burdensome for the ISP whereas considerations on the right of information and personal data were additional so that it is not clear to what extent those rights alone may have been seriously infringed by a filtering system. Furthermore, in the following case *SABAM v Netlog*[145] the CJEU gave a judgement very similar to *Scarlet v SABAM* whereas it could have elaborated more on users rights. In fact, the case dealt with an injunction imposing a filter with the same characteristics of the one in *Scarlet v SABAM* on all information stored by a hosting service provider (Netlog). However, whereas Scarlet offered internet access, Netlog was running an online social networking platform which allowed registered users to have a space, communicate with friends and publish contents such as personal photos. Also in this judgment, the CJEU concluded that such an injunction 'may'[146] infringe protection of personal data or the right of information and did not develop a deep reasoning on the level of protection of those rights.[147] However, filtering a social network should involve more attention on freedom of expression and information since it could be more difficult to avoid blocking lawful content.

[144] See, among others, Harris, O'Boyle, Warbrick (2014) 522ff.

[145] C-360/10, *Belgische Vereniging van Auteurs, Componisten en Uitgevers CVBA (SABAM) v Netlog NV*, ECLI:EU:C:2012:85.

[146] Ibid., para 48.

[147] In this regard see also Mylly (2015) at 117.

Concerning the reasoning on the measure consisting in cutting access to internet in *Mc Fadden v Sony* the CJEU stated that there would have been a serious infringement of freedom to conduct business, and this sufficed to affirm that no fair balance was struck, without making any reference to freedom of information of internet users. Although a WiFi close to a shop has a different value compared to home internet connection, open WiFis are much used so that the CJEU could have at least mentioned that the national judge could have assessed also users' rights. Hopefully, the CJEU will have the possibility to clarify whether and to what extent the EU acknowledges a right to access to internet given that the Council of Europe and the United Nations are promoting it[148] and given that the issue is very sensitive for the legitimacy of IPRs, as critics of the 'three strike test' showed.[149] The importance of an EU harmonized response stems also from the fact that recently a Spanish Court of Appeal ordered an ISP to cut off internet access to one of its subscribers alleged of engaging in P2P file sharing on the basis of art. 8.3 Information Society Directive.[150]

Analogous considerations can be made with regard to the protection of personal data of the users. In *Scarlet* the CJEU affirmed that IP addresses are personal data[151] but did not clarify under which principles the collection and identification of users addresses should be operated in the event of filtering systems. However, it could have made reference to the provisions of the Directives on the processing of personal data[152] or to art. 7 and 8 EUCFR, as AG Cruz Villalón did[153] (for example, according to the European Data Protection Supervisor indiscriminate monitoring of internet

---

[148] Human rights Council, *Resolution on the Promotion, Protection and Enjoyment of Human Rights on the Internet* (27 June 2016) UN Doc A/HRC/32/L.20, para 10; Council of Europe, *Recommendation to Member States on Measures to Promote the Public Service Value of the Internet*, n. 16, 7 November 2007; Parliamentary Assembly, *The Right to Internet Access*, resolution 1987, 9 April 2014. In general see, among others, S Tully (2014).

[149] See para 1.

[150] Promusicae et al. v. R Cable y Telecomunicaciones Galicia, SA, Barcelona Court of Appeals, Judgment 470/2013, 18 December 2013. For a comment see Husovec, Peguera (2015) 21ff.

[151] C-70/10 *Scarlet* (n 44), para 51. See also case C-582/14, *Patrick Breyer v Bundesrepublik Deutschland*, ECLI:EU:C:2016:779, para 49.

[152] Directive 95/46/EC (n 55); Directive 2002/58/EC (n 49).

[153] Opinion of Advocate General Cruz Villalón in case C-70/10, *Scarlet Extended SA v Société belge des auteurs, compositeurs et éditeurs SCRL (SABAM)* [2011] ECR I-11959, paras 69ff.

users, for all the activities in P2P networks, for infringements not of commercial scale are disproportionate and violate art. 8 EUCFR).[154]

Also, concerning the measure consisting in password-protecting an internet connection in *Mc Fadden*, no consideration of privacy protection has been made while the CJEU could have referred to art. 8 ECHR and art. 8 EUCFR. In this regard, AG Spuznar underlined that this obligation entails 'a need to identify users and to retain their data'[155] which amounted to a disproportionate administrative constraints in the case of a seller offering internet access as a secondary activity.[156]

Overall, it therefore emerges that the CJEU should pay more attention on freedom of information and protection of personal data in order to strike a fair balance among all involved fundamental rights. Otherwise, the fundamental rights reasoning will not be able to enhance the legitimacy of IPRs in the EU legal order and to achieve the desired 'renewed consensus'.[157] Furthermore, from the broader human rights perspective, the mentioned drawback of inflation of human rights seems likely[158] and if, on the one hand, a case-by-case assessment based on the proportionality principle guarantees the adequate balance in the specific case, on the other hand relying on proportionality may undermine legal certainty and raises the need for the role of the legislator.[159] Having said that, it is also true that, on the merit, the CJEU findings are not so unbalanced: filtering systems and cutting internet access have not been allowed and the outcome online blocking injunction may be considered as balanced. More doubtful is the measure consisting in password-protecting internet access.

It is also necessary to make more general considerations on the recourse to the EUCFR by the CJEU. The fact that when member states implement EU rules they must apply those rules in accordance with

[154] Opinion (n 119), para 25.
[155] Opinion of Advocate General Spuznar in case C-484/14, *McFadden* (n 101) para 140.
[156] Ibid., para 142.
[157] See para 2.
[158] See para 2. For a deeper analysis of human rights' inflation see J Mchangama, G Verdirame, *Human Rights Inflation*, Freedom Rights Project, http://www.freedomrights.info/wp-content/uploads/2013/07/HR-Inflation.pdf.
[159] See F Fontanelli, (2015) and Peukert (2015) at 132-48.

fundamental rights has been affirmed by the Court in the 80s.[160] Now, the EUCFR applies primarily to the institutions and bodies of the Union and "to the member states only when they are implementing Union law" (art. 51.1 EUCFR) and the notion of "implementing" has been interpreted in a broad manner[161] so that the CJEU's reasoning on balancing fundamental rights in *Promusicae* and in the following judgments analyzed above, has to be considered in this framework.

However, the Charter does not extend the EU competences (according to art. 6.1 TEU and art. 51.2 EUCFR) and, in this regard, the fact that after *Promusicae* the CJEU left the deferential approach and went into detail on whether a balance among fundamental rights was struck[162] may be seen as exceeding the EU competences, for example if one considers that, according to Directive 2001/29 and to Directive 2004/48, conditions and modalities of injunctions should be left to national law.[163] At the same time, this would be a very restrictive interpretation of art. 51.2 EUCFR which is not supported by relevant case-law.[164]

Furthermore, the Charter does not restrict or adversely affect human rights as recognized by EU law, international law or other international agreements to which the EU or all member states are party, in particular the ECHR, and member states Constitutions (art. 53 EUCFR). This raises the question whether the national judge is allowed to ensure higher protection, for example, for freedom of expression and the right to personal data than the one granted in the judgments analyzed above. However, the CJEU set a broad limit in this regard since 'national authorities and courts remain free to apply national standards of protection of fundamental rights, provided that the level of protection provided for by the Charter, as interpreted by the Court, and the primacy, unity and effectiveness of EU

[160] Case 5/88, *Hubert Wachauf v Bundesamt für Ernährung und Forstwirtschaft*, ECLI:EU:C:1989:321, para 19 on which see Tridimas (n 33) at 320ff.

[161] See case C-617/10, *Åklagaren v Hans Åkerberg Fransson*, ECLI:EU:C:2013:105 para 28 and, for a more comprehensive analysis A Ward (2014) 1433ff.

[162] See para 3. The same trend concerns not only IPRs case-law but also other cases such as case C-544/10, *Deutsches Weintor eG v Land Rheinland-Pfalz*, ECLI:EU:C:2012:526.

[163] See Directive 2001/29 recital 59 (n 21) and Directive 2004/48 recital 23 (n 21).

[164] See C-617/10, *Åklagaren* (n 161) and case C-40/11, *Yoshikazu Iida v Stadt Ulm*, ECLI:EU:C:2012:691.

law are not thereby compromised'.[165] It has therefore to be seen whether the desirable interplay between the CJEU and national judges will be possible in this field.[166] At the moment, only in *UPC Telekabel* the CJEU affirmed that inconsistency of an online blocking injunction not imposing specific measures with freedom of information should have been assessed by the national judge whereas it could have done the same also in *Netlog* and in *McFadden v Sony*, as mentioned. Whereas concerning the right to personal data the interplay appears rather difficult considering the broadening of the EU competence in this field so that hopefully the CJEU will take it more into account.

In conclusion, this ever-expanding jurisdiction is another element that makes crucial the need for the CJEU to develop more the reasoning on freedom of expression and the right to personal data.[167]

6. AN EU *SUI GENERIS* SYSTEM OF HUMAN RIGHTS PROTECTION

From the analysis of the case-law above it also emerges that the EU is shaping a *sui generis* system compared to the international human rights law.

Overall, it has to be underlined a general different feature of international law compared to the EU system where the EUCFR has been defined as a 'prelude to a European Constitution'.[168] In fact, although the interactions between international economic law and international human rights law have been intensely discussed, as shows the known Alston-Petersmann debate,[169] it can be affirmed that they are still distinct fields if one consider the World Trade Organization agreements, including the

[165] See case C-399/11, *Stefano Melloni v Ministerio Fiscal*, ECLI:EU:C:2013:107, para 60.

[166] On the interplay between the CJEU and national judges see, among others, de Witte, (2014), at 1533-38 and Rauchegger (2015).

[167] On the expanding jurisdiction and legitimacy it is also interesting to refer to a old debate in J Coppel, A O'Neill, (1992) and JHH Weiler, NJS Lockhart, (1995).

[168] K Lenaerts, E De Smitjter, (2001) 298.

[169] EU Petersmann, (2002a); P Alston, (2002); Petersmann (2002b). More recently see Wager, Watal, (2015) 149ff.

TRIPs, and the so-called International Bill of Human Rights system. In this framework, it has not to be assumed *a priori* that international economic law is inconsistent with human rights, especially ICESCR (Desierto, 2015, p. 160) and it cannot be argued that respects for human rights prevails on the protection of IPRs in the event of a conflict since, looking at the enforcement mechanisms of the two fields, it appears that international economic law has stronger mechanisms.

More specifically, the fact that IPRs and freedom to conduct business have the same status of other human rights is critical from the perspective of international human rights law.

Concerning IPRs it has been mentioned that their human rights nature can stem from the UDHR's right to property but the Covenants do not provide a similar provision and, also concerning the authors' protection of moral and material interests resulting from their works, the Committee on Economic, Social and Cultural Rights clarified that this 'does not necessarily coincide' with IPRs legislation.[170] The analyzed EU judgments concern copyright (for the moment case law on trademarks did not refer to human rights[171]), which may be closer to the protection of moral and material interests of the authors (art. 15.1.c ICESCR) but hopefully the Committee will further address this issue. In fact, it is not clear which scientific, literary or artistic production qualify for human rights protection under art. 15 ICESCR (Haugen, 2007, p. 66). Furthermore, protection should be accorded to economic interests that 'contribute to the enjoyment of the right to an adequate standard of living'[172] (art. 11, para 1 ICESCR) and therefore the scope of the material interests protected under human rights should be narrower than that of property (Beiter, 2008, p. 717) but there is no guidance on how to shape human rights protection and no

---

[170] See para 1.

[171] Joined Cases C-236/08 to C-238/08, *Google France SARL and Google Inc. v Louis Vuitton Malletier SA* (C-236/08), *Google France SARL v Viaticum SA and Luteciel SARL* (C-237/08) *and Google France SARL v Centre national de recherche en relations humaines (CNRRH) SARL and Others* (C-238/08) [2010] ECR I-2417; C-324/09, *L'Oréal* (n 121). See also A Marsoof, '(2015); Reiss, (2011) 185-87.

[172] General Comment 17 (n 14) para 15.

relevant case-law at international level.[173] Finally, art. 15.1.c ICESCR should be seen in the broader context of art. 15 which ensures cultural rights and also on this balance clarifications are needed.[174] In light of these considerations, the CJEU should better clarify the contents of IPRs as a fundamental rights compared to previous IPR legislation.

Concerning freedom to conduct business, although this could be recognized in art. 6 ICESCR, i.e., 'the right of everyone to the opportunity to gain his living by work which he freely chooses or accepts' (which is also present in the European Social Charter as 'the right of the worker to earn his living in an occupation freely entered upon' (art. 1.2)), it can be affirmed that it does not have solid roots on international human rights instruments. At the same time, the fact that it is not a human right does not mean that intermediaries' interests are not protected, as also the ECtHR jurisprudence shows.[175] Therefore, it is desirable to have more guidance at international level also on this freedom.

The lack of sources of international human rights law on freedom to conduct business was among the reasons that made the inclusion of it in the EU Charter controversial (Everson, Correia Gonçalves, 2014, p. 438). The fact that 'freedom' to conduct a business has to be exercised 'in accordance with Union law and national law and practices' seems to 'raises an assumption that its exercise is limited, by contrast to right to work and property' (Everson, Correia Gonçalves, 2014, p. 444). In this regard, the CJEU affirmed that it can be subject to 'a broader range of interventions on the part of public authorities which may limit the exercise of economic activity in the public interest'.[176] Furthermore, 'it would be reasonable to expect that individuals and smaller businesses would in practice benefit the most, as even small infringements of the right are likely to have a relatively larger impact on them'.[177] At the moment *McFadden v Sony* dealt with an individual pursuing an economic activity,

[173] B Saul, D Kinley, J Mowbray, *The international covenant on economic, social and cultural rights: commentary, cases and materials* (Oxford University Press 2014).
[174] Report of the Special Rapporteur in the field of cultural rights (n 17); C Geiger (2016).
[175] See para 4.
[176] C-283/11, *Sky Österreich GmbH v Österreichischer Rundfunk*, ECLI:EU:C:2013:28, para 46.
[177] Freedom to conduct a business: exploring the dimensions of a fundamental right, (European Union Agency for Fundamental Rights, 2015) 11.

although of secondary nature[178] but also in *Scarlet* freedom to conduct a business prevailed on IPRs enforcement and there is case law in other fields such as on the balance of the rights of employees with the employer's freedom to conduct a business[179] and the balance with the right to health:[180] hopefully future case law will better clarify the role of art. 16.

A further critical issue is the possibility of corporations to invoke human rights instruments. The fact that big corporations like Google can benefit from human rights protection of intellectual property and freedom to conduct business led to a debate on whether this should be allowed or whether human rights should be destined only to natural persons.[181] It is not possible to further the question here but it has to be underlined that under the ICCPR corporations had standing only under restrictive conditions (S Joseph, M Castan, (2013) 76-78) while the ECHR system and the EUCFR are more open to legal persons.[182]

Finally, the CJEU should have made more reference to human rights instruments in the analysed case-law[183] (which is a more general problem[184]), especially concerning freedom of expression and personal data protection. At the same time, also regarding them it would be desirable to have more guidance concerning the aspects related to the digital environment and, in particular, on their relationship with IPRs, for example concerning anonymity on the internet.[185]

---

[178] See para C.

[179] C-426/11, *Mark Alemo-Herron et al. v Parkwood Leisure Ltd*, ECLI:EU:C:2013:521.

[180] C-544/10, *Deutsches* (n 162).

[181] See, among others, Janewa OseiTutu (2015) 40ff; Helfer, Austin (2011) 61-64; Yu, (2007) 1124ff. More in general see Ku, The Limits of Corporate Rights Under International Law http://chicagounbound.uchicago.edu/cgi/viewcontent.cgi?article=1627&context=cjil 746ff.

[182] In this regard see van den Muijsenbergh, Rezai, Corporations and the European Convention on Human Rights http:// www.mcgeorge.edu/Documents/Conferences/GlobeJune2012_Corporationsandthe.pdf 48ff.

[183] See for example Opinion of Advocate General Cruz Villalón in case C-70/10, (n 153) para 82.

[184] De Burca underlines a 'remarkable lack of reference on the part of the Court of Justice to other relevant sources of human rights law and jurisprudence' (De Burca, (2013) 173).

[185] In this regard see Report of the Special Rapporteur on the right to privacy, Joseph A. Cannataci (8 March 2016) UN Doc A/HRC/31/64; Report of the Special Rapporteur A/HRC/17/27 (n 7). And specifically on anonymity see Report of the Special Rapporteur on the promotion and protection of the right to freedom of opinion and expression, David Kaye (22 May 2015) UN Doc A/HRC/29/32.

CONCLUSION

The relationship between online piracy and human rights is a fascinating and challenging topic. The EU approach to deal with IPRs enforcement based on striking a balance among involved fundamental rights does not seem to have enhanced IPRs legitimacy yet and critical aspects appear from the broader perspective of the international human rights system. Overall, it strongly emerges the need for guidance from decision-makers at the EU and at international level, also to prevent a privatization of enforcement inconsistent with the rights of users.[186]

In this framework, recent EU initiatives are to be welcomed. In fact, the Commission issued a proposal for the modernisation of copyright in the digital single market[187] and a proposal for the modernisation of regulation on protection of personal data in electronic communications.[188] Although a provision that would impose a filtering system has already been much criticized,[189] hopefully these proposals will reopen a constructive debate and will bring a legislation capable of shaping the adequate balance among the interests of all involved actors. In particular, the crucial link between enforcement measures and a balanced definition of the notion of online piracy has to be carefully looked at. The CJEU recently had the possibility to consider whether hyperlinks, i.e., clickable internet links redirecting users to press article and photographs protected by copyright, constitute a communication to the public under Directive 2001/29.[190] Moreover, in the

[186] Hins, Hugenholtz, McGonagle, van Daalen, van Hoboken, Angelopoulos, Brody, Margoni, Study of fundamental rights limitations for online enforcement through self-regulation (Technical Report), 2016, http://www.ivir.nl/publicaties/download/1796.

[187] Proposal for a Directive of the European Parliament and of the Council on copyright in the Digital Single Market COM(2016)593.

[188] Proposal for a Regulation concerning the respect for private life and the protection of personal data in electronic communications and repealing Directive 2002/58/EC (Regulation on Privacy and Electronic Communications) COM(2017)10.

[189] EDRI, Deconstructing Article 13 of the Copyright proposal of the European Commission, https://edri.org/files/copyright/copyright_proposal_article13.pdf. See also Summary of results of the public consultation on the future of electronic commerce in the internal market and the implementation of the directive on electronic commerce, http:// ec.europa.eu/ internal_market/consultations/docs/2010/e-commerce/summary_report_en.pdf, 13-14.

[190] Directive 2001/29 (n 21). See C-160/15, *GS Media BV v Sanoma Media Netherlands BV and Others*, 8 September 2016.

near future the Court will judge on the act of indexing the metadata related to files containing copyright-protected works offered on P2P networks in the case concerning The Pirate Bay website.[191] Setting a balanced notion of copyright and an exclusive rights balanced with adequate exceptions is therefore essential not to prejudice the legitimacy of enforcement measures. Hopefully the proposal to modernise copyright will go in this direction.

REFERENCES

Alston, P. (2002). Resisting the merger and acquisition of human rights by trade law: a reply to Petersmann. *European Journal of International Law*, *13*, 815-44.

Beiter, D. (2008). The Right to Property and the Protection of Interests in Intellectual Property - A Human Rights Perspective on the European Court of Human Rights' Decision in Anheuser-Busch Inc. v. Portugal. *International review of intellectual property and competition law*, *39*, 714-21.

Benedek, W. & Kettemann, M. C. (2013). *Freedom of expression and the internet*. Council of Europe.

Chapman, A. R. (2002). The Human Rights Implications of Intellectual Property Protection. *Journal of International Economic Law*, *5*, 861-82.

Çoban, A. R. (2004). *Protection of property rights within the European convention on human rights*. Aldershot: Ashgate.

Coppel, J. & O'Neill, A. (1992). The European Court of Justice: Taking Rights Seriously? *Common Market Law Review*, *29*, 669-92.

Cornides, J. (2004). Human Rights and Intellectual Property, Conflict or Convergence? *The Journal of World Intellectual Property*, *7*, 135-67.

[191] See Opinion of Advocate General Szpunar in Case C-610/15 (n 75).

De Burca, G. (2013). After the EU Charter of Fundamental Rights: The Court of Justice as a Human Rights Adjudicator? *Maastricht J. Eur. Comp. L.*, *20*, 168-184.

de Witte. (2014). Article 53. In S. Peers, T. Hervey, J. Kenner, A. Ward (eds) *The EU Charter of Fundamental Rights*, *A Commentary*. Oxford, Portland: Hart Publishing.

Desierto, D. (2015). Public Policy in International Economic Law, The ICESCR in Trade, Finance and Investment. Oxford: Oxford University Press.

Drahos, P. (1998). The universality of intellectual property rights: origins and development. In WIPO, OHCHR (eds), *Intellectual property and human rights*, (pp. 13-42). http://www.wipo.int/edocs/pubdocs/en/intproperty/762/wipo_pub_762.pdf.

Everson, Correia Gonçalves. (2014). Article 16. In S. Peers, T. Hervey, J. Kenner, A. Ward (Eds), *The EU Charter of Fundamental Rights*, *A Commentary*. Oxford, Portland: Hart Publishing.

Fontanelli, F. (2015). The Mythology of Proportionality in Judgments of the Court of Justice of the European Union on the Internet and Fundamental Rights. *Oxford Journal of Legal Studies*, *36*, 630-60.

Fuster, G. G. (2014). The emergence of personal data protection as a fundamental right of the EU, Springer.

Garstka, K. K. (2012). The Amended Digital Economy Act 2010 as an Unsuccessful Attempt to Solve the Stand-Alone Complex of Online Piracy, *International review of intellectual property and competition law*, *43*, 158-74.

Geiger, C. (ed.) (2016). Intellectual Property and Access to Science and Culture: Convergence or Conflict?, ICTSD.

Geiger, C. (ed) (2015). Research Handbook on Human Rights and Intellectual Property. Cheltenham, Northampton: Edward Elgar.

Geiger, C. (2011). Honourable Attempt but (ultimately) Disproportionately Offensive against Peer-to –peer on the Internet (HADOPI) – A Critical Analysis of the Recent Anti-File-Sharing Legislation in France. *International review of intellectual property and competition law*, *42*, 457-72

Geiger, C. (2009). Intellectual Property Shall be Protected!? –Article 17(2) of the Charter of Fundamental Rights of the European Union: a Mysterious Provision with an Unclear Scope., *European Intellectual Property Review*, *31*, 113-17.

Geiger, C. (2006). Constitutionalising" Intellectual Property Law? The Influence of Fundamental Rights on Intellectual Property in the European Union. *International review of intellectual property and competition law*, *37*, 371-406.

Griffiths, J. & McDonagh, L. (2013). Fundamental rights and European IP law: the case of Art 17(2) of the EU Charter. In C. Geiger (ed.), Constructing European Intellectual Property, Achievements and new perspectives Cheltenham, Northampton: Edward Elgar.

Grosheide, W. (ed.), (2010). Intellectual Property and Human Rights: a Paradox. Cheltenham, Northampton: Edward Elgar.

Harris, D. J., O'Boyle M. & Warbrick, C. (2014). Law of the European Convention on Human Rights (2 edn). Oxford: Oxford University Press.

Haugen, H. M. (2007). General comment No. 17 on "authors' rights". *The Journal of World Intellectual Property*, *66*, 53-69.

Haugen, H. M. (2005). Intellectual Property-Rights or Privileges? *The Journal of World Intellectual Property*, *10*, 445-58

Helfer, L. & Austin, G. W. (eds) (2011). Human Rights and Intellectual Property: Mapping the Global Interface. Cambridge: Cambridge University Press.

Helfer, L. (2008). The New Innovation Frontier? Intellectual Property and the European Court of Human Rights. *Harvard Int'l Law Journal*, *49*, 1-52.

Hilty, R., Kur, A. & Peukert, A. (2006). Statement of the Max Planck Institute for Intellectual Property, Competition and Tax Law on the Proposal for a Directive of the European Parliament and of the Council on Criminal Measures Aimed at Ensuring the Enforcement of Intellectual Property Right. *International review of intellectual property and competition law*, *37*, 970-77.

Horten, M. (2012). The Copyright Enforcement Enigma, Internet Politics and the 'Telecoms Package'. Palgrave.

Husovec, M. & Peguera, M. (2015). Much Ado about Little – Privately Litigated Internet Disconnection Injunctions. *International review of intellectual property and competition law*, *37*, 10-37.

Janewa OseiTutu, J. (2015). Corporate "Human Rights" to Intellectual Property Protection? *Santa Clara L. Rev.*, *55*.

Joseph, S. & Castan, M. (2013) *The international covenant on civil and political rights: cases, materials, and commentary* (3 edn). Oxford: Oxford University Press.

Lenaerts, K. & De Smitjter, E. (2001). A "Bill of rights" for the European union. *Common Market Law Review*, *38*, 273-300.

Marsoof, A. (2015). The Blocking Injunction – A Critical Review of Its Implementation in the United Kingdom Within the Legal Framework of the European Union. *International review of intellectual property and competition law*, *46*, 632-64.

Matulionyte, R. (2011). ACTA's Digital Chapter: remaining concerns and what can be done. *Queen Mary Journal of Intellectual Property*, *1*, 248-71.

Mylly, T. (2015). The constitutionalization of the European legal order: Impact of human rights on intellectual property in the EU. In C. Geiger (ed), Research Handbook on Human Rights and Intellectual Property. Cheltenham, Northampton: Edward Elgar.

Mylly, T. (2005). Intellectual property and fundamental rights: do they interoperate? In N. Bruun (ed.), Intellectual property beyond rights WSOY.

Oetheimer. (2012). Art. 10(I). In Bartole, S., De Sena, P., Zagrebelsky V. (Eds), Commentario breve alla Convenzione europea dei diritti dell'uomo. Padova: Cedam.

Petersmann, E. U. (2002a). Time for a United Nations 'Global Compact' for Integrating Human Rights into the Law of Worldwide Organizations: Lessons from European Integration. *European Journal of International Law*, *13*, 621-50.

Petersmann, E. U. (2002b). Taking Human Dignity, Poverty and Empowerment of Individuals More Seriously: Rejoinder to Alston. *European Journal of International Law*, *13*, 845-51.

Peukert, A. (2015). The fundamental right to (intellectual) property and the discretion of the legislature. In C. Geiger (ed), *Research Handbook on Human Rights and Intellectual Property*. Cheltenham, Northampton: Edward Elgar.

Peukert, A. (2012). Why do 'good peple' disregard copyright on the internet?. In C Geiger (ed.), Criminal enforcement of intellectual property: a handbook of contemporary research. Cheltenham, Northampton: Edward Elgar.

Rauchegger, (2015). The Interplay Between the Charter and National Constitutions after *Åkerberg Fransson* and *Melloni*, Has the CJEU Embraced the Challenges of Multilevel Fundamental Rights Protection?. In de Vries, Bernitz, Weatherill (eds), *The EU Charter of Fundamental Rights s a Binding Instrument.* Hart Publishing.

Raustiala, K. (2007). Density and Conflict in International Intellectual Property Law. *UC Davis L. Rev.*, 1021-38.

Reiss, J. W. (2011). Commercializing Human Rights: Trademarks in Europe After *Anheuser-Busch v Portugal. The Journal of World Intellectual Property*, *14*, 176-201.

Savola, P. (2014). Proportionality of Website Blocking: Internet Connectivity Providers as Copyright Enforcers. *JIPITEC*, *5*, 116-38.

Schabas, W. (2015). The European Convention on Human Rights, A Commentary. Oxford: Oxford University Press.

Schneider, M. & Vrins, O. (2012). The Magnitude and the Economic and Social Consequences of Counterfeiting and Piracy. In O. Vrins, M. Schneider (Eds), Enforcement of Intellectual Property Rights through Border Measures, Law and practice in the EU (2nd edn). Oxford: Oxford University Press.

Schutte, C. B. (2004). The European Fundamental Right of Property. Kluwer.

Tyler, T. R. (1997). Compliance with intellectual property laws: a psychological perspective. *New York University J. Int'L. Policy*, *29*, 219-36.

Torremans, P. (2014). Article 17(2) In S. Peers, T. Hervey, J. Kenner, A. Ward (eds), The EU Charter of Fundamental Rights, A Commentary. Oxford, Portland: Hart Publishing.

Torremans, P. (ed.) (2008). Intellectual property and human rights: enhanced edition of Copyright and human rights. Alphen aan den Rijn: Kluwer Law International.

Tridimas, T. (2006). The general principles of EC law (2nd edn). Oxford: Oxford University Press.

Tully, S. (2014). A Human Right to Access the Internet? Problems and Prospects. *Human Rights Law Review*, *14*, 175-95.

Ubertazzi, L. (2007). IP and the Draft Treaty on the European Union. *International review of intellectual property and competition law*, *38*, 881-83.

Van Eecke, P. (2011). Online service providers and liability: A plea for a balanced approach. *Common Market Law Review*, *48*, 1455-1502.

Verbiest, Spindler. & Riccio, Van der Pierre. (2007). Study on the liability of internet intermediaries http://ec.europa.eu/internal_market/e-commerce/docs/study/liability/final_report_en.pdf.

Waelde, C., Brown, A., Kheria, S. & Cornwell, J. (2016). Contemporary Intellectual Property, Law and Policy (4th edn). Oxford: Oxford University Press.

Wager, Watal. (2015). Human rights and International intellectual property law. In C. Geiger (ed.) Research Handbook on Human Rights and Intellectual Property. Cheltenham, Northampton: Edward Elgar.

Ward, A. (2014). Article 51. In S. Peers, T. Hervey, J. Kenner, A. Ward (eds), *The EU Charter of Fundamental Rights*, *A Commentary*. Oxford, Portland: Hart Publishing.

Weiler, J. H. H. & Lockhart, N. J. S. (1995). Taking Rights Seriously" Seriously: The European Court and its Fundamental Rights Jurisprudence. *Common Market Law Review*, *32*, 579-627.

Woods. (2014). Article 11. In S. Peers, T. Hervey, J. Kenner, A. Ward (eds). The EU Charter of Fundamental Rights, A Commentary. Oxford, Portland: Hart Publishing

Yu, P. (2007). Reconceptualizing Intellectual Property Interests in a Human Rights Framework. *UC Davis L. Rev.*, *40*, 1039-1149.

In: European Union
Editor: Wilbert Strickland
ISBN: 978-1-53612-359-3

Chapter 4

CRITICS OF THE CATALAN INDEPENDENCE PROCESS AND CATALAN POLITICAL NATIONALISM

David Ramiro Troitino, Archil Chochia, and Tanel Kerikmäe
Tallinn University of Technology, Tallinn, Estonia

ABSTRACT

The article analyzes Spain's internal conflict over the breakaway intentions of a part of Catalonian society, going through different influential aspects such as history, ethnicity, language and culture; economy, the structure of the Spanish central government, the role of European Union and several other milestones in the main claims of the supporters of the independence for Catalonia. The research disputes the nationalistic idea through a unionist perspective, arguing the supranational character of the Spanish state. In addition the writing draws attention to the fact that there is distortion between the physical area influenced by Catalan culture and the much smaller region of the political movements supporting the independence.

Keywords: Catalonia, Spain, nationalism, independence, right to decide, multinational state, supranational state

INTRODUCTION

This article analyses the on-going conflict between Catalonia and the Spanish state, laying out different pillars in order to understand the most problematic parts of the matter and its political implications in main human areas - politics, economy and culture.

The situation itself is new neither for Spain nor for the rest of Europe: creation of new states based on national claims has been a political issue here since the end of the XIX century, generating numerous conflicts and wars as in Ukraine today. Of course all these conflicts always had other components and external influence factors, but the roots remained the same. The tendency towards a growing new wave of nationalism in many parts of Europe also had its effect on the situation escalating in Catalonia. As for all the member states inside the European Union which have experienced the contradictions of a region trying to become an independent state, for Spain too this means pressure - on one hand for the state to share more sovereignty on the European level and on other to face a regions increasing demands for national sovereignty on an inner, regional level; the latter always doing so inside the Union, accepting and promoting its federal scope.

Focusing on analysing different aspects of the national political claims of a sector of Catalan society, this research attempts to dismantle the main arguments of those supporting the creation of a new state. From a humanist scientific perspective the current multi-cultural society is based on political ideas linked with the concept of citizenship rather than nationality. In the light of the European building process or the integration of the world economy in current globalization, instead of atomizing our societies more, the international situation invites to unite.

History

The arguments of having an ancient Catalan nation cannot be explained from historical point of view. Historically different peoples, folks and nations have populated the territory that currently is Spain. During the period before the arrival of Greek and Romans to the Iberian Peninsula, the inhabitants were divided into several main groups and tribes; particularly Iberians, Basques, Celtíberians and Celts. The Iberians were located in all the Mediterranean coast of the Spanish peninsula, from the north border with the Pyrenees till Gibraltar, including the Atlantic coast in the south. The Basques were mainly populating the area of the current Basque country (including the French Basque areas) and partly the region of Navarra. The Celtíberians, a mix of Celts and Iberians were living in the central areas of the territory and finally, the Celts occupied mainly the northwest of the peninsula. Hence, there were no peoples, tribes or cultural groups forming the one Catalan nation, like for example the Basques can state being the only cultural group in Spain that has kept its identity since ancient times (Llobera, 1983).

The Roman conquer of the area divided the territory to different provinces, originally to the Hispania Citerior and the Hispania Ulterior, and at the end of the Roman Empire into Tarraconense, Gaelicia, Cartaginense, Balearica, Betica y Lusitania. These administrative divisions of the Iberian Peninsula during the Roman rule can be slightly identified with some cultural groups, such as Betica with Andalusia or Gaelicia with the current Galicia; and these administrative territories still match with some Spanish official regions, such as Balearica with Balearic Islands nowadays. The concept of Catalonia, however, did not exist. The territory of the current Catalonia was mostly included in the Tarraconense province that was a much wider territory, stretching from the Mediterranean to the Atlantic (Nogué, 2014).

The Barbarian invasions during the collapse of the Roman Empire included several barbaric tribes and folks: the Visigoths, Suevis, Vandals and Alans. None of these ethnical groups were anyhow identified with the Catalan territory. They gradually merged with the local population, mainly composed by Hispano-Romans including the important emigration from Italy during the centuries of the Roman rule, the local population assimilated to the Roman culture. Again, the only outstanding exception were the Basque, who surprisingly kept their national identity thanks to the rugged terrain, the absence of prominent cities (with the exception of Pamplona) and its peripheral situation within the Roman Empire. Territorial organization linked with the barbarian invasions, that in other parts of Europe were the genesis of numerous nations, does not take place either - there is still no trace of any Catalan cultural, ethnical group (Martínez-Herrera, 2002).

During the Muslim conquer of the peninsula most of the territory became part of Al-Andalus state, including the majority of the current territory of Catalonia, whereas some areas of Northern Spain such as Asturias, the Basque country and the small county of Aragon, were independent Christian political units. The northern part of current Catalonia soon became a part of the Frankish Empire, a buffer territory to stop the Muslim expansion, in a unit known as the Spanish Mark, which included all the southern border of the Pyrenees. The local population of the Mark was diverse, including Iberians, Hispano-Romans, Basques, Jews and Goths who had been conquered or subjugated by the Muslim Caliphate of the Umayyad. The territory changed with the feudal ambitions of those appointed to administer the counties (López, 1983). Eventually the lack of a strong central power, difficulties in the communication system and the long process of collapse of the Frankish Empire after the death of Charles the Great, lead to the rulers and people of Mark becoming autonomous and claiming independence, creating different semi-autonomous feudal territories, germs of the states of Navarra and Aragon, parts of current Catalonia being included to both.

The following - Christian states expanding southwards - meant the end to the presence of Muslims as political actors in the peninsula and eventually led to the creation of Spain. The union of the Kingdoms of Castile, Aragon and the annexation of Navarra, plus the territories won over from the Muslims, meant the creation of Spain in 1512 (Cárcel 2013). The populations of these states had their own cultural structures, often divided in several sub-cultural groups with individual dialects, but all of them were mainly local Christians and immigrants from the rest of Europe: France, Italy and Germany - the Christians were expelling the Muslims southwards and huge portions of the territory were completely empty. Therefore, there was no dominant ethnical group creating the Spanish identity or the Catalonian identity. In terms of languages all the area was originally using Latin as the main language (Laitin, 1985), and the local dialects, which indeed, afterwards became languages; Castilian, Galician or Catalan among others, with the exception of the Basque again, that kept its language and cultural traditions over all these historical periods (Moreno, 1998).

Conclusion

1. Catalonia has never been an independent political structure. Hence the idea of regaining the independence is not sustainable historically.
2. Catalonia has never existed as a compact historical territory before the creation of Spain, diversity inside Catalan territories was a historical constant.
3. The region of Spanish Catalonia was a part of the Kingdom of Aragon of its own free will, without any military occupation, besides the feudal conflicts common in all Europe.
4. Aragon united to Castile of its own free will, by the marriage of the King Fernando of Aragon and the queen of Castile Isabel.
5. Spain was the consequence of a political and dynastic union of different territories and folks, plus the military occupation of the last Muslim Kingdom of the peninsula, and the Kingdom of Granada, whose inhabitants were forced to leave the peninsula.

Spain is the union of different peoples, traditions, languages and it is populated by a heterogenic ethnic group, a consequence of the previous occupations of the territory and newcomers from Christian Europe. Spain cannot be understood without any part that participated in this union; if any element breaks away, what is known as Spain will stop existing.

ETHNICITY

Before the Roman times, different Iberian tribes, mainly Ausetanos, Ilergetes, Ilercaones and others populated the current territory of Catalonia. They shared their main cultural values with the rest of the population of the Mediterranean coast of the Iberian Peninsula, and the wars between tribes were common. So, as these tribes belonged to the Iberian culture, spread all over the Peninsula, especially in the coastal areas of the Mediterranean, no original Catalan ethnical group linked with one specific ancient folk existed.

The Mediterranean soon became a communication hub, so there were important movements of population in the current territory of Catalonia. Phoenicians and Greeks founded their own trade emporiums and cities, trying to keep their identity with little integration to the local population. Nevertheless, when the Romans arrived and started controlling the Greek colonies all over the Mediterranean, they inherited the conflicts between Greek and Phoenicians and afterwards Carthaginians. The Romans did assimilate to the local population creating a new dominant group, but that group did not correspond with Catalonian people as an ethnical group either, since it was spread all over the coastal area of the Peninsula (Muñoz, 2013).

As mentioned, the collapse of the Roman Empire meant the arrival of Visigoths, Suevis, Vandals and Alans, who also mixed with the local population after the end of the segregation system established in the first period of the occupation. That segregation had mostly been based on ethnic and religious beliefs - Germanic people were mainly following Arianism and the local population Roman Catholicism. Nevertheless, the barbarians did not inhabit only the current territory of Catalonia, they had a much bigger scope, including for example, a vast extension to the Southern France (Smith, 2014).

The arrival of Muslims meant a movement of population reluctant to convert to Islam from the south to the north of the Iberian Peninsula, to live under a Christian ruler and also, movement from the Christian territories in the north of Europe looking for new lands where to settle in the south of Europe.

Later on, after one of the numerous internal conflicts of Spain, the new King Philip V introduced a concept of a central state, central market and unity in the country by the Nueva Planta laws. This concept increased the internal mobility of the Spanish population as the internal borders gradually disappeared, integrating the Spanish population more and more. This process speeded up once again on the XX century, when people moved massively from Southern Spain towards Catalonia to work, as important industries of the area were in bad need to cheap labour. The ethnical melting pot of the territory was vigorous, the integration of these southern Spanish workers and their families became an important part in the cultural essence of Catalonia as well (Etherington, 2014).

It is difficult to give an assessment to the data on the ethnic composition of states, nevertheless Professor Isajiw from the University of Toronto, has calculated that out of a total of 189 states analysed, 150 include four or more ethnic groups, and only two countries (Iceland and Japan) list just one ethnical group (Isajiw, 1974). This would put Spain, consisting mostly of just one ethnical group all over its territory, to a rather exceptional position in the current world...

Hence we can conclude that from an ethnical point of view:

- All the population movements that affected the current Catalonia also affected the rest of the Iberian Peninsula. Hence the ethnical group in the nowadays Catalonia is exactly the same than in the rest of the Spanish territory.
- All the Spanish, with the different cultural groups, different languages and different history, belong to the same ethnical group, once more with the exception of the Basques - but yet the Basque ethnicity influence in Castile is very important.

LANGUAGE

On current territory of Catalonia different languages have been spoken during different historical periods. The main language before the Roman occupation was Iberian, without any trace of a local dialect being exclusive on the territory of Catalonia nowadays, but many dialects based on tribal organization. During the Greek expansion over the Mediterranean the Greek language became the main language of the area, substituted by Latin during the Roman period.

The current Catalan language originates from the local Latin dialect, as most of the Spanish languages - like Galician or Castilian for example. The Basque language is the only unique one: since its roots are pre-Iberian, it is not even included in the Indo-European language family. In other words, besides the Basque, all these languages are daughters of the same mother and share most of its essence. Perhaps Catalan does have some influence from Occitan language (from the south of France) because of the political connection of the territory during the Frankish domination (Johnston, 1991), but then again as a consequence of the physical location and the political influences, there are many dialects inside the Catalan language itself. We cannot actually speak about a sole Catalan language as a distinctive sign of nationality.

The nationalist movement of XIX century created a normative Catalan though, that is currently accepted all over the Catalan territory and other regions of Spain: Valencia, Balearic Islands; including even some parts of southern France. Hence the territory of the current Catalonia cannot be identified with the linguistic area of the Catalan language. Catalan language, as Castilian, Basque and Galician, is currently recognized as an official language of the Spanish state (Conversi, 1990).

There are around 7,000 languages, 5,000 ethnic groups and just under 200 states in the world (Llobera, 1995). It means that the average quantity of languages in a state is no less than 35, and in Europe the average of languages by country is 4.6 per state. It is estimated that there are only 25 linguistically homogeneous states in the world. In most states, not only several, but dozens or even hundreds of languages are spoken. Catalonian language shares its territorial influence with other languages as Spanish, French or Italian.

As a conclusion of a linguistic analysis, the territorial sphere of influence of the Catalan language does not match with the political borders of the region of Catalonia. Hence this region or political entity cannot claim a political independence and the creation of its own national state based on language premises, unless it includes all these territories where Catalan language is spoken - where the support to the Catalan nationalism is minimal... (Payne, 1971).

CULTURAL ASPECTS

Catalonia does not represent a unique culture focus on a specific territory because it owns a wider scope that includes some parts of the south of France, some areas of the Spanish region of Valencia, the eastern part of the region of Aragon and also the region of Balearic Islands. Nevertheless there is a common culture that the Catalans identify with. The Catalan culture is divided downwards in different regional subcultures and local entities, and it is a basic element upwards in the creation of the Spanish culture, which was created from the contributions of different cultural groups included in the Spanish territory (Anderson, 2014). The work of any outstanding Spanish artist cannot be understood without the Catalan contribution: the works of Dali include many Spanish elements, the work of Picasso - an artist from southern Spain, who also lived in Barcelona - is highly influenced by Catalonia. Hence the Spanish culture is based on the huge richness of the country in terms of different cultural groups, an exchange of influences, and the Catalan culture cannot be understood without the cultural relations with other regions of Spain (Hargreaves, 2000). Sure, the cultural aspects of Catalonia give an identity to the regions population, but it is created from many different subcultures and regional differences and is an important part of a wider culture - the Spanish culture. The Catalan nationalists try to decrease the importance of the regional and local differences of the Catalan culture and increase the differences with the Spanish culture, presenting it as an alien to the Catalan community, instead of a fusion of the different cultures inside the Spanish territory. Catalonian government is acting as France with its internal differences, creating the nation from the state, and as Germany with the relations with Spain, trying to create the state from the nation (Fichte, 2006). The contradiction hampers the nationalist credibility.

NATIONALISM

The concept of nationalism is based on the concept of a nation, a group of humans sharing their cultural aspects. The identification of political and cultural aspects is something relatively recent from the XIX century, when national states became the centre of the political arena. The right of self-determination supported by the American president Wilson after the I WW could be called an opening of a new era in the world history, even though this right was applied just according to the interest of the allies, as we can see in case of Hungary, the Balkans and other areas of Europe (Sans, 2011).

Nationalism focuses on a group rather than citizens, as the political rights come from belonging to a nation, not from belonging to a society. Hence you belong to a society because you belong to a cultural group - those who do not share the national cultural values or do not accept the predominance of the nation over the society do not have space in the public life of the national state.

One of the main pillars of nationalism is ethnicity, independence is sought when an ethnical group living in a state dominated by another ethnical group, feels discriminated or disaffected of the common cultural values imposed by the dominant group. In case of Catalonia there are no ethnical reasons for the creation of a different state as the Catalan ethnical group does not exist, it is the same than the Spanish ethnical group (Jeram, 2014).

As mentioned, the cultural and linguistic aspects of Catalonia are controversial too. The culture is different inside Catalonia, and also it is an important part of the Spanish culture; there is no clear distinction between Catalonian culture and Spanish culture. The language goes far beyond the territory of the current Catalonia. Hence the claim for a national Catalonian state is difficult to support from both cultural and linguistic point of view (Conversi, 1995).

Based on centralistic ideas Catalan nationalism unites different subcultures inside its area of influence and then artificially breaks the links and separates the Catalan culture from the Spanish culture, creating borders inside a melting pot that is consequence of common living during centuries. Spain is a nation of nations, a supranational state where, according to the article 2 of the Spanish constitution, the Spanish nation is made by the nations and regions of Spain. The idea of the Spanish nation as a Matryoshka doll is the essence of the Spanish state. The Spanish nationality is made by the regional, provincial, county and local identity of the citizens. The sum of all these factors creates a new concept, the Spanish nation, enriching all members with a new level of identity. Spain is diverse, but also Catalonia is, with strong local and regional identities. The Catalan nationalists are keen accepting and promoting the diversity inside the Spanish state as a milestone in their claims for political independence, but refuse to see its own diversity asking for respect, that apparently is not willing to bestow (Woolard, 1989).

Economy and Taxes

In economic terms Catalonia is one of the most developed areas of Spain, but these economic developments cannot be understood without the concept of Spain.

First, the creation of Spain meant the creation of a Spanish market with high custom taxes to foreign products in order to increase local development. The mercantilism or economic nationalism was adopted, clearly favouring the economic development of the region of Catalonia, that basically had the monopoly of the Spanish market for its manufactures (Castells, 2014).

The industrial development of Catalonia cannot be understood without the massive contribution of other parts of Spain in terms of population - new industries there needed cheap labour which mainly came from the South of Spain, allowing the companies located in Catalonia to keep high productiveness and even export their production to other European states, mostly France. This movement of population was inducted by the Catalan industrialists rather than the Spanish central government (Giner, 1980).

The income per capita in Catalonia is higher than in most of Spain, with the exception of Madrid, the Basque Country and Navarra. According to the Spanish tax system the citizens contribute to the society via taxes according to their income, hence the contribution of Catalonia has been higher than other regions. The Spanish central state spends this money on public services and public investment in infrastructures all over Spain - as the system is based on solidarity, less developed areas of the state have bigger benefits than their contribution to the common budget in order to help them grow (Viu, 1998). In fact, this has been the main complaint of the Catalan nationalists supporting the independence during several decades: the unfairness of the system (i Permanyer, 1977), Catalonia contributes more than receives. It is commonly perceived as a clear discrimination all over the territory of Catalonia, and also a great part of the rest of the Spanish, even though it sounds absurd. First of all, the territories do not pay taxes, the individual citizens and companies according to their income do. It is not that all the Catalans pay the same just because they are a cultural group of Catalans - the citizens with higher incomes pay more and the citizens with lower incomes pay less (Muñoz, 2014).

There lies a clear contradiction to the idea that Spain is unfair: the complaint about the taxation forgets the idea of solidarity on the state level, whereas on local, Catalan level and on a wider level of European Union it is supported. According to this logic Barcelona as the richest part of Catalonia would probably feel discriminated in an independent Catalonia because they would pay more than the rest of the new country, and receive less than other more poor areas (Resende, 2014). And finally it is absolutely overlooking the fact, that the region that pays more taxes than any other and has the biggest difference between the amount paid and the investments received from the central state is Madrid, not Catalonia.

THE SPANISH STATE

The current Spanish state was founded after the death of Franco and the 40 years of dictatorship, on federal basis. The degree of autonomy of the different Spanish regions is one of the highest in Europe. In case of Catalonia it means creation of its own institutions, specially a regional parliament and a president with wide powers (Guibernau, 2004).

Because of linguistic reasons Catalonia also has its own police forces (as the agents need to speak Catalan to communicate with the citizens whose native language is Catalan), Catalan language as official language in all public institutions and complete autonomy in the educational field, where Catalan is the vehicular language. Besides that Catalonia has powers over such strategic fields as the health care system, communications with its own public TV and radio channels, etc. (Carreras, 2013). All this makes the claims of cultural discrimination and hence the idea of discrimination being the reason to split up the state, simply illogical, populist and completely unsustainable - the Catalan culture is highly protected.

So far the Western world has built democracies on cultural homogeneous populations, but modern states unite citizens, not nations. It is a process that is being enforced by international tendencies: the European Union (Ramiro, 2008), integration, globalization. The Spanish state itself is an example of the new world situation. It includes several nations, sub-nations and an amazing cultural and regional diversity internally, and is involved in the construction of a European supranational political structure externally. This kind of complexity links an individual - the citizen - stronger to the public affairs; the organization of the states, rather than the organisation of the political life based on national principles.

The Spanish state structure respects the individual freedom of the citizens, providing same rights to all of those holding it, regardless of their cultural affinity or cultural group, playing a supranational role, avoiding exclusion of those who do not fully identify themselves with a specific national group; the miscegenation character of the nations in Spain makes their cultural boundaries blurred, so it is a large number. The pretention of building a state in Catalonia based on national principles would lead to the discrimination of all of those not fully committed to the Catalan nation cause (Shabad, 1982).

The European Union

Spain is a member of the European Union, any territory that becomes independent automatically stops being a part of the Union. Hence, an independent Catalonia would be out of the European Union and more importantly, out of the European Common Market, out of the freedom of movement for people and economic agents. It would affect strongly the Catalan economy and its main source of incomes: tourism. Catalan companies are focused on the external market, selling most of its production outside the territory of Catalonia. Being out of the European Market would affect their economic capacity enormously, leading to a remarkable crisis until substitute markets would be found, if achievable (Ramiro, 2013).

Spain, France, UK and other countries with national minorities would block Catalonia to access to the European Union because it is a threat to their own existence: it would settle a dangerous example for other regions of Europe; besides, for any enlargement of the European Union unanimity is required. This means the independence of Catalonia would certainly lead the territory into a significant economic crisis (Whitmeyer, 2002).

On cultural aspects globalization is not just moving capital or merchandises, but also people, languages, religions and cultures. There are around 200 million emigrants all over the world, counting for more than 20% of the total population in Paris, 30% in London, 40% in New York and more than 50% in Toronto, Vancouver or Miami. Barcelona, the main city of Catalonia, counts with more than 40 minority linguistic and cultural groups. Cultural diversity is a fact, regardless of our feelings, and the European Union is powering this diversity (Ramiro, 2014). The number of Europeans travelling to and living in Catalonia, especially Barcelona and the Mediterranean coastal areas, increases this diversity and the European essence of Catalonia. There is a great contradiction between the Catalan nationalism and the aim towards sharing different levels of identity - Catalan and European, rejecting the same premise on Spanish level, when the latter obviously roots of centuries of cohabitation (Rendon, 2007).

The Right to Decide

These days Catalonia is focused on the call for a regional referendum to ask how the citizens feel about the independence of Catalonia, trying to follow the example of Scotland (Bourne 2014). But the case of Catalonia is very different. Who and on what basis has the right to decide? Does the answer derive from an ethnical group, a cultural nation, a political society, a historic idea, a social group, the citizens or is it a combination of all the previous factors? (Swenden, 2014).

It is also important to define the timeline. How often could these referendums be held? In Scotland (Keating, 1997), the supporters of the independence have already declared that they will try another time in the close future. Should the referendums for the independence be held each 30 years, 5 years, each month or each day until the result is favourable? (Roller, 2003).

In terms of politics the modern world has abdicated to implement the French tradition of building a cultural nation homogenising the population, respecting the diversity as something positive enriching the society. Thus the nations, cultural groups, should also reject the previous position based on the German model, according to which each nation should be transformed into a State and the Wilson doctrine (Tilly, 1975).

The main difference between the Catalans and the rest of the Spanish is the language, but if being a common linguistic and cultural group (being a nation) would give the right to decide, then in practise it would mean three options: homogenising the population into a national standard, ethnic purity or adapting the number of states to the number of nations (Guibernau, 2000) This would create thousands of states in the world, making international relations a boiling matter clashing with the ongoing globalization.

The right to decide based on national roots should be granted just for those discriminated (Kerikmäe, 2013) or under a violent assimilation from a state, or those without any possibilities of participating in political life on equal terms with the rest of the citizens. None of it applies on Catalonia.

The right to decide is given to all the citizens living in the region of Catalonia and those born there, but living abroad. The petition does not include the people of other territories where Catalan cultural influence and Catalan nation is present, mainly Valencia and Balearic Islands (Oltra, 2014), creating another contradiction - should the right to decide be granted to the territory or to the nation?

Conclusion

1. Catalonia is a part of Spain and one cannot truly understand either without the other. If Catalonia becomes an independent state, Spain will become something different.
2. The Spanish and Catalonian history is common.
3. The Spanish State includes Catalonia, other cultural regions and other different national groups, Spain is the sum of its cultural diversity.
4. Most of the languages come from the same root, Latin.
5. The Spanish culture is the same all over the territory of the state; it is a culture created by the union of different cultures, each territory has its own cultural variations and differences.
6. The Catalan nationalism is exclusionary and is based on the idea of belonging to a nation. On the other hand the Spanish state is based on the idea of solidarity and equality of the citizens in political terms, no matter to which national group they belong.

7. Taxes are paid by individual persons and companies, not by territories. Benefits are shared based on solidarity.
8. The Catalan economy depends on the Spanish market and vice versa.
9. When European states are uniting in a supranational organization, the nationalists of Catalonia want to separate on national grounds.
10. The right to decide is not universal to any group of people. It has to be backed by important reasons, such as cultural discrimination, ethnical threats or violent assimilation, facts that do not apply in the Catalan case.

All in all the current political conflict between the Catalan government and the Spanish government is artificial. It is based on sectarian opinions and emotions rather than facts and has huge potential negative effects for the people by dividing the citizens of Catalonia and Spain into two confronting groups – the believers of the Catalan nationalist movement and the supporters of the Spanish diversity.

Acknowledgments

The authors would like to thank Mercedes Samaniego, Jean Monnet Professor, and the anonymous reviewers for their helpful comments and suggestions.

References

[1] Anderson, Lara. "The unity and diversity of La olla podrida: an autochthonous model of Spanish culinary nationalism." *Journal of Spanish Cultural Studies* ahead-of-print (2014): 1-15.
[2] baron de Montesquieu, Charles de Secondat. *The Politcal Theory of Montesquieu*. CUP Archive, 1977.

[3] Bourne, Angela K. "Europeanization and Secession: The Cases of Catalonia and Scotland." *JEMIE* 13 (2014): 94.

[4] Castells, Antoni. "Catalonia and Spain at the crossroads: financial and economic aspects." *Oxford Review of Economic Policy* 30, no. 2 (2014): 277-296.

[5] Cárcel, Ricardo García. "Los mitos de la historia de España" [The myths of the history of Spain]. *Humanidades* 40 (2013): 67-70.

[6] Carreras Serra, Francesc de. "Reflexiones sobre la propuesta de nuevo Estatuto de Cataluña" [Reflections on the proposal for a new Statute of Catalonia]. *Teoría y realidad constitucional* 16 (2013): 43-82.

[7] Conversi, Daniele. "Language or race?: The choice of core values in the development of Catalan and Basque nationalisms." *Ethnic and Racial Studies* 13, no. 1 (1990): 50-70.

[8] Conversi, Daniele. "Reassessing current theories of nationalism: nationalism as boundary maintenance and creation." *Nationalism and Ethnic Politics* 1, no. 1 (1995): 73-85.

[9] Díez Medrano, Juan. "Naciones dividas (clase, política y nacionalismo en el País Vasco y Cataluña)" [Divided nations (class, politics and nationalism in the Basque Country and Catalonia] *Monografías* (1999).

[10] Etherington, John. "Catalonia since the Spanish Civil War: reconstructing the nation." *Ethnic and Racial Studies* ahead-of-print (2014): 1-2.

[11] Fichte, Johann Gottlieb. *Fichte: addresses to the German nation*. Cambridge University Press, 2008.

[12] Giner, Salvador. *The social structure of Catalonia*. No. 1. Anglo-Catalan Society, 1980.

[13] Guibernau, Montserrat. "Nationalism and intellectuals in nations without states: the Catalan case." *Political Studies* 48, no. 5 (2000): 989-1005.

[14] Guibernau, Montserrat. *Catalan nationalism: Francoism, transition and democracy*. Routledge, 2004.

[15] Hargreaves, John. *Freedom for Catalonia?: Catalan Nationalism, Spanish Identity and the Barcelona Olympic Games*. Cambridge University Press, 2000.

[16] i Permanyer, Borja de Riquer, and Josep Fontana i Lázaro. *Lliga regionalista: la burguesia catalana i el nacionalismo (1893-1904)* [Regionalist League: Catalan bourgeoisie and Nationalism (1893-1904)]. 1977.

[17] Isajiw, Wsevolod W. "Definitions of Ethnicity." *Ethnicity* 1, no. 2 (1974): 111-124.

[18] Jeram, Sanjay. "Sub-state Nationalism and Immigration in Spain: Diversity and Identity in Catalonia and the Basque Country." *Ethnopolitics* 13, no. 3 (2014): 225-244.

[19] Johnston, Hank. *Tales of nationalism: Catalonia, 1939-1979*. Rutgers University Press, 1991.

[20] Keating, Michael. "Stateless nation-building: Quebec, Catalonia and Scotland in the changing state system." *Nations and nationalism* 3, no. 4 (1997): 689-717.

[21] Keating, Michael. "Class, Sector and Nation. Support for Minority Nationalism Among Peak Interest Groups in Four Western European Countries." *Territory, Politics, Governance* 2, no. 3 (2014): 322-337.

[22] Kerikmäe, Tanel. *Protecting human rights in the EU: controversies and challenges of the Charter of Fundamental Rights*. Springer Science and Business Media, 2013.

[23] Laitin, David D. "Linguistic revival: Politics and culture in Catalonia." *Comparative Studies in Society and History* 31, no. 02 (1989): 297-317.

[24] Llobera, Josep R. "The idea of Volksgeist in the formation of Catalan nationalist ideology." *Ethnic and Racial Studies* 6, no. 3 (1983): 332-350.

[25] Llobera, Josep R. *Culturas, estados, ciudadanos: una aproximación al multiculturalismo en Europa* [Cultures, states, citizens: an approach to multiculturalism in Europe]. Edited by Emilio Lamo de Espinosa. Alianza Editorial, 1995.

[26] López, Astrid Barrio. "Organización y papel político del nacionalismo moderado catalán durante la Transición." In: *Los partidos en la Transición: las organizaciones políticas en la construcción de la democracia española* [The parties in the Transition: political organizations in the construction of Spanish democracy], pp. 307-322. Biblioteca Nueva, 2013.

[27] Martínez-Herrera, Enric. "From nation-building to building identification with political communities: consequences of political decentralisation in Spain, the Basque Country, Catalonia and Galicia, 1978-2001." *European Journal of Political Research* 41, no. 4 (2002): 421-453.

[28] Moreno, Luis, Ana Arriba, and Araceli Serrano. "Multiple identities in decentralized Spain: The case of Catalonia." *Regional and Federal Studies* 8, no. 3 (1998): 65-88.

[29] Muñoz, Juan Antonio Inarejos. "Nacionalismos e identidades en la enseñanza de la historia de España: avances y resistencia" [Nationalisms and identities in the teaching of Spanish history: advances and resistance]. *Clío* 39 (2013): 32-12.

[30] Muñoz, Jordi, and Raül Tormos. "Economic expectations and support for secession in Catalonia: between causality and rationalization." *European Political Science Review* (2014): 1-27.

[31] Nogué, Joan, and Joan Vicente. "Landscape and national identity in Catalonia." *Political Geography* 23, no. 2 (2004): 113-132.

[32] Oltra, Lluís Català. "Discursos polítics sobre la identitat territorial en els partits valencians d esquerra i de centreesquerra" [Political discourse on territorial identity in the parties of left and center-Valencia]. *Papers: revista de sociología* 99 (2014): 187-212.

[33] Payne, Stanley. "Catalan and Basque nationalism." *Journal of Contemporary History* (1971): 15-51.

[34] Payne, Stanley G. "Nationalism, regionalism and micronationalism in Spain." *Journal of Contemporary History* (1991): 479-491.

[35] Rendon, Silvio. "The Catalan premium: language and employment in Catalonia." *Journal of Population Economics* 20, no. 3 (2007): 669-686.

[36] Sans, Xavier Torres. *Naciones sin nacionalismo: Cataluña en la monarquía hispánica (siglos XVI-XVII)* [Nations without nationalism: Catalonia in the Hispanic monarchy (XVI-XVII centuries)]. Universitat de València, 2011.

[37] Ramiro Troitino, David. "De Gaulle and the European Communities." *Proceedings of the Institute for European Studies* 4 (2008): 139-152.

[38] Ramiro Troitino, David. "The Current Economic Crisis of the EU: Genesis, Analysis and Solutions." *Baltic Journal of European Studies* 3, no. 1 (2013): 6-28.

[39] Ramiro Troitino, David. "The British Position towards European Integration: A Different Economic and Political Approach." *Baltic Journal of European Studies* 4, no. 1 (2014): 119-136.

[40] Resende, Madalena Meyer. *Catholicism and Nationalism: Changing Nature of Party Politics*. Routledge, 2014.

[41] Roller, Elisa, and Pieter Van Houten. "A national party in a regional party system: The PSC-PSOE in Catalonia." *Regional and Federal Studies* 13, no. 3 (2003): 1-22.

[42] Shabad, Goldie, and Richard Gunther. "Language, nationalism, and political conflict in Spain." *Comparative Politics* (1982): 443-477.

[43] Smith, Angel. *The Origins of Catalan Nationalism, 1770-1898*. Palgrave Macmillan, 2014.

[44] Swenden, Wilfried, and Nicole Bolleyer. "Regional Mobilization in the New Europe: Old Wine in a New Bottle?." *Regional and Federal Studies* 24, no. 3 (2014): 383-399.

[45] Tilly, Charles. "Reflections on the history of European state-making." *The formation of national states in Western Europe* (1975): 3-83.

[46] Tura, Jordi Solé. *Nacionalidades y nacionalismos en España: autonomías, federalismo, autodeterminación* [Nationalities and nationalisms in Spain: autonomies, federalism, self-determination]. Alianza Editorial, 1985.

[47] Viu, Vicente Cacho. *El nacionalismo catalán como factor de modernización* [Catalan nationalism as a factor of modernization]. 1998.

[48] Whitmeyer, Joseph M. "Elites and popular nationalism*." *The British journal of sociology* 53, no. 3 (2002): 321-341.

[49] Woolard, Kathryn Ann. *Double talk: Bilingualism and the politics of ethnicity in Catalonia*. Stanford University Press, 1989.

INDEX

A

access, 6, 13, 24, 35, 39, 44, 46, 47, 48, 49, 51, 52, 53, 55, 59, 61, 62, 63, 90
accessibility, 57, 59
aggression, 14, 15, 18, 20
arbitration, 60
Archil, v, 11, 77
assessment, 63, 83
assimilation, 92, 93
authorities, 24, 25, 42, 49, 50, 51, 54, 57, 64, 67
autonomy, 28, 89

B

Balkans, 22, 86
banking, 56
bankruptcy, 5, 7
banks, 4
Belgium, 15
benefits, 9, 16, 21, 88
blocking injunctions, 49

C

capital controls, 3
capitalism, vii, viii, 1, 2, 4, 5, 7, 8
Capitalism, v, 1
case law, 37, 42, 58, 66, 68
Catalonia, viii, ix, 77, 78, 79, 80, 81, 82, 83, 84, 85, 86, 87, 88, 89, 90, 91, 92, 93, 94, 95, 96, 97, 98
censorship, 50, 60
Central African Republic, 26
Charter of Fundamental Rights of the European Union, 39, 72
child pornography, 38, 50
China, 8, 9, 19, 24, 25
circulation, 8, 37
citizens, vii, viii, 1, 2, 4, 5, 9, 25, 27, 86, 87, 88, 89, 91, 92, 93, 95
citizenship, 78
civil action, 60
civil society, 35
Civil War, 13, 26, 94
Cold War, viii, 11, 12, 13, 14, 15, 19, 21, 22, 24, 27, 28, 29, 30, 31
commerce, 38, 69

commercial, 14, 37, 54, 59, 63
Common Foreign and Security Policy, 22
Common Market, 13, 17, 24, 29, 31, 70, 73, 75, 90
communication, 15, 50, 52, 69, 80, 82
communism, 13, 14, 15
communist countries, 18
community, viii, 11, 12, 17, 18, 20, , 21, 28, 29, 86, 96
compensation, 58
competing interests, 50
competition, 15, 24, 43, 70, 71, 72, 73, 75
competitive ability, 7
conflict, viii, ix, 17, 20, 21, 22, 23, 27, 42, 66, 77, 78, 93, 97
confrontation, 12, 19, 26
consensus, 29, 37, 39, 63
consent, 31, 47, 52, 58
construction, 89, 96
contradiction, 86, 88, 91, 92
controversial, 35, 38, 67, 86
cooperation, 14, 16, 17, 23, 26, 27
copyright, 34, 38, 45, 47, 48, 49, 51, 53, 55, 57, 59, 66, 69, 74
Council of Europe, 46, 62, 70
Council of the European Union, 49
counterfeiting, 34, 37, 41, 54
crises, vii, viii, 1, 3, 7
cultural influence, 92
cultural tradition, 81
cultural values, 82, 86
culture, viii, ix, 16, 37, 77, 78, 80, 82, 85, 86, 87, 89, 92, 95
currency, 7, 8
customers, 44, 45, 47, 52

D

de Gaulle, Charles, 19
decentralisation, 96
defence, 13, 15, 16, 18, 19, 29
democracy, vii, viii, 1, 4, 5, 9, 26, 50, 94, 96
Democratic Capitalism, 5
denial, vii, viii, 1, 3
Denmark, 20, 21
discrimination, 38, 88, 89, 90, 93
diversity, 81, 87, 89, 91, 92, 93
domestic conflict, 28

E

economic activity, 13, 43, 53, 67
economic crisis, 90
economic development, 17, 21, 23, 87
economic performance, 14, 23
economic problem, 13
ECSC, 14, 18
Eisenhower, Dwight David, 15
electronic communications, 38, 43, 44, 69
emerging markets, 3
emigration, 80
empire of law, 12
employees, 68
employment, 7, 8, 96
enforcement, ix, 33, 34, 37, 38, 39, 41, 44, 48, 51, 52, 54, 56, 57, 58, 59, 66, 68, 69, 74
enlargement, 21, 23, 90
environment, 4, 35, 61, 68
EPC, 19
Estonia, 11, 22, 23, 60, 77
ethnic groups, 83, 84
ethnicity, viii, ix, 77, 83, 86, 98
EU Charter of Fundamental Rights, 39, 71, 74, 75, 76
Europe, vii, viii, 1, 3, 5, 8, 10, 13, 16, 17, 19, 20, 21, 22, 23, 25, 26, 27, 28, 29, 37, 54, 58, 74, 78, 80, 81, 83, 84, 86, 89, 90, 95, 97
European Central Bank (ECB), 7
European Commission, 21, 24, 37, 39, 69
European Community, 13, 14

European Court of Human Rights, viii, ix, 33, 39, 57, 70, 72
European Court of Justice, 70
European integration, 2, 16, 17, 19, 29, 30, 31
European international relations, 12
European market, 23, 24
European Parliament, 18, 21, 27, 35, 37, 38, 39, 50, 56, 69, 72
European Union, v, vii, viii, ix, 1, 2, 7, 11, 12, 13, 14, 17, 21, 22, 25, 26, 27, 28, 33, 35, 37, 39, 41, 56, 61, 67, 71, 72, 73, 75, 77, 78, 88, 89, 90, 91
European Union Foreign Affairs, 12
EU-Russia, 12
EU-US relations, 12
evidence, 55, 59
exercise, 43, 67
external action, 12, 23, 26
external relations, 14, 15, 31

F

Federal Republic of Yugoslavia, 31
Federal Reserve, 4
federalism, 18, 20, 28, 97
filtering system, 45, 46, 61, 62, 63, 69
financial crisis, vii, viii, 1, 2, 3, 5, 7, 8, 13, 26
financial markets, 6
financial resources, 47
force, 17, 18, 24, 25, 28, 36, 49
foreign affairs, 12, 20, 23, 28, 30
fragmentation of governance, 9
France, viii, 11, 12, 14, 15, 18, 19, 20, 26, 58, 59, 66, 71, 81, 82, 84, 85, 88, 90
freedom of expression, ix, 33, 34, 37, 38, 43, 46, 48, 50, 58, 59, 60, 61, 64, 65, 68
Freedom of information, 43
freedom to conduct business, 34, 37, 43, 45, 46, 47, 53, 60, 61, 62, 66, 67, 68

G

genocide, 38
Germany, viii, 7, 11, 12, 13, 14, 15, 18, 20, 21, 52, 53, 56, 81, 86
globalization, 24, 78, 89, 90, 92
Google, 41, 49, 51, 66, 68
governance, 2, 9, 28, 29, 30
governments, 2, 5, 6, 7, 17, 22
Great Britain, 3, 9
Greece, 7, 15, 21
guidance, ix, 19, 34, 46, 49, 66, 67, 68, 69

H

health care system, 89
hegemony, 14
history, viii, ix, 12, 21, 28, 36, 77, 83, 86, 92, 94, 96, 97
hostility, 38
housing, 4, 6, 8
human rights, viii, ix, 25, 33, 34, 36, 37, 40, 41, 48, 50, 63, 64, 65, 66, 67, 68, 69, 70, 71, 73, 75, 95
Hungary, 7, 23, 60, 86

I

Iceland, 83
identification, 46, 54, 62, 86, 96
identity, 58, 79, 81, 82, 85, 87, 91, 96
IMF, 7
income, 4, 6, 88
independence, viii, ix, 17, 29, 77, 78, 80, 81, 85, 86, 87, 88, 90, 91
Independence, v, 77
individuals, 36, 44, 67
industrialized countries, 34
industries, 34, 54, 83, 88
inequality, 4, 6

inflation, 3, 7, 8, 9, 40, 63
infrastructure, 2
injunction, 38, 44, 45, 46, 47, 48, 51, 52, 53, 54, 61
institutions, 18, 19, 21, 24, 64, 89
integration, 12, 15, 16, 17, 18, 21, 23, 24, 78, 82, 83, 89
intellectual property, viii, ix, 33, 34, 36, 37, 38, 39, 40, 42, 43, 45, 47, 53, 54, 55, 56, 57, 58, 68, 70, 71, 72, 73, 74, 75
interest rates, 4
interference, 43, 51, 57, 59, 60
intermediaries, 38, 41, 50, 67, 75
International Covenant on Civil and Political Rights, 49
International Covenant on Economic, Social and Cultural Rights, 36
international law, ix, 34, 41, 64, 65
International Monetary Fund, 7
international relations, 12, 19, 24, 92
Internet Service Providers, 38
investments, vii, viii, 1, 5, 89
issues, 16, 17, 19, 21, 35, 39
Italy, 7, 15, 33, 80, 81

J

Japan, 35, 56, 83
jurisdiction, 25, 65

K

Keynes, vii, viii, 1, 3, 5, 6
Keynes, John Maynard, vii, viii, 1, 5
Keynesian, 5, 6, 7, 8
Keynesian theory, 6, 7, 8
Keynesian tradition, 5
Keynesianism, 2, 3
Keynesians, vii, viii, 1
knowledge economy, 34
Korea, 35, 39, 56

L

languages, 81, 83, 84, 90, 92
Latvia, 22, 23
laws, 43, 75, 83
lead, ix, 18, 33, 41, 45, 48, 51, 80, 90
leadership, 15, 19, 20
legislation, 21, 24, 25, 36, 39, 40, 55, 56, 66, 69
liberalization, 4, 6
light, vii, ix, 33, 37, 41, 44, 59, 67, 78
Lithuania, 22, 23
litigation, 56
living conditions, 9
loans, 2, 4, 6, 7, 8
lying, vii, ix, 11

M

majority, 9, 17, 18, 80
management, 16, 44, 47, 60
market economy, 8
materials, 51, 67, 73
matter, 4, 37, 78, 92
Mediterranean, 7, 79, 82, 84, 91
melting, 6, 83, 87
mercantilism, 87
methodology, 12
military, 15, 16, 18, 19, 20, 26, 81
military occupation, 81
Min, Ho Chi, 15
minorities, 22, 90
Moldova, 58
monetary policy, 7
monopoly, 5, 87
Morocco, 35, 56
multiculturalism, 95
multinational state, 22, 78
Muslims, 80, 83

N

national debt, vii, viii, 1, 3
national identity, 80, 96
national interests, 22
nationalism, 9, 16, 78, 85, 86, 87, 91, 92, 93, 94, 95, 96, 97, 98
nationalists, 85, 87, 88, 93
nationality, 78, 84, 87
NATO, 19, 20, 23, 26
negative effects, 93
Netherlands, 14, 15, 40, 69
neutral, 14, 21
New Zealand, 35, 56
Nobel Prize, 8
North America, 13, 19, 29, 30, 31
nuisance, 55
nutrition, 29

O

OECD, 34
officials, 30
online blocking injunction, 48, 63, 65
online piracy, vii, ix, 33, 34, 35, 37, 41, 54, 57, 69
operations, 15, 26

P

Parliament, 39, 56, 57
password, 52, 53, 54, 63
password-protecting an internet connection, 53, 63
Paul Krugman, 8
peace, vii, ix, 11, 12, 14, 17, 20, 21, 22, 23, 27
piracy, vii, ix, 33, 34, 35, 37, 41, 54, 57, 69
playing, viii, 11, 90
policy, vii, viii, 1, 3, 6, 7, 8, 15, 17, 19, 29, 37
policymakers, 3
political aspects, 18
political instability, 22
political party, 39
political power, 4
political system, 13, 21
politics, vii, viii, 2, 4, 8, 9, 14, 15, 16, 20, 78, 91, 94, 98
poor politics, 2
population, 6, 23, 26, 79, 80, 82, 83, 85, 88, 90, 91, 92
Portugal, 5, 7, 15, 21, 57, 70, 74
predictability, 25
prejudice, 49, 70
President, 2, 5, 8, 9, 15, 19, 44, 86, 89
principles, vii, viii, 1, 5, 8, 9, 42, 62, 75, 89, 90
privatization, vii, viii, 1, 3, 69
privatized loans, 6
property rights, 34, 35, 70
proportionality, 42, 43, 49, 55, 63
proportionality principle, 42, 49, 63
protection, ix, 33, 35, 36, 37, 38, 40, 43, 44, 45, 46, 48, 51, 54, 55, 56, 57, 60, 61, 62, 63, 64, 66, 68, 69, 71
protection of personal data, ix, 33, 37, 43, 45, 55, 61, 62, 63, 69
public affairs, 89
public domain, 34
public interest, 16, 58, 67
public investment, 88
public life, 86
public loans, 7, 8
public policy, 28, 29, 30
public service, 88
publishing, 55
purchasing power, 7

R

Rajan, G. Raghuram, 3
real estate, 4, 6, 7, 60
realism, 31
reality, 6, 18, 51
reasoning, ix, 33, 37, 42, 61, 62, 63, 64, 65
Red Army, 13
reform, 20, 21, 27
regionalism, 96
Regulation, 2, 10, 30, 37, 56, 69
regulations, 2, 5, 7, 9
regulatory framework, 38
religious beliefs, 82
resistance, 16, 96
resolution, 3, 35, 62
resources, 19, 51
response, 8, 26, 31, 38, 62
right of information, 46, 54, 55, 56, 61
right to decide, 78, 91, 92, 93
right to personal data, 34, 42, 64, 65
rights, ix, 25, 33, 34, 35, 36, 37, 38, 40, 41, 42, 43, 44, 45, 46, 48, 49, 51, 52, 54, 55, 56, 57, 59, 60, 61, 62, 63, 64, 66, 67, 68, 69, 70, 72, 73, 75, 86, 89
Romania, 19, 23, 57
roots, 67, 78, 84, 91, 92
rule of law, 58
rules, 24, 25, 63
Russia, 8, 12, 21, 24, 27

S

sanctions, 38
scope, 12, 36, 43, 58, 66, 78, 82, 85
Second World, 3
security, 23, 29, 31
segregation, 82
self-regulation, 50, 69
service provider, 48, 52, 61, 75
services, 8, 24, 31, 38, 39, 44, 48, 54, 55
social acceptance, 39
social class, 13
social consequences, 34
social group, 91
social network, 61
social problems, 6, 13
social psychology, 29
social structure, 94
society, viii, ix, 26, 38, 44, 58, 59, 60, 77, 78, 86, 88, 91
solidarity, 88, 92, 93
solution, vii, viii, 1, 3, 4, 5, 8, 13, 18
sovereignty, 17, 18, 19, 20, 21, 23, 26, 28, 78
Soviet Union, viii, 11, 14, 15, 20, 21
Spain, viii, ix, 5, 7, 13, 15, 21, 25, 77, 78, 79, 80, 81, 83, 84, 85, 87, 88, 90, 92, 93, 94, 95, 96, 97
stability, 3, 14, 17, 21, 23
stabilization, 13
stagflation crisis, 3, 6
stakeholders, 39
state intervention, 3
states, vii, viii, 2, 7, 9, 11, 13, 16, 17, 18, 20, 21, 22, 23, 25, 26, 52, 56, 63, 64, 78, 80, 83, 84, 86, 88, 89, 92, 93, 94, 95, 97
structure, viii, ix, 18, 77, 81, 89
supranational state, 78, 87
Supreme Court, 57, 60
Sweden, 14, 21, 39, 55, 58, 59
Switzerland, 40
synthesis, 40

T

taxes, 87, 88
territorial, 85, 96
territory, 21, 22, 23, 79, 80, 81, 82, 83, 84, 85, 87, 88, 90, 92
terrorism, 30, 38
the combination crisis, 8

theoretical approach, 17
trade, 9, 13, 24, 25, 39, 70, 82
trade agreement, 9, 39
trade union, 9
trademarks, 34, 66
transmission, 52, 58
Trump, Donald, 2, 9
Turkey, 49, 51

U

Ukraine, 78
unemployment rate, 7
United Kingdom, viii, 11, 13, 15, 21, 50, 58, 73
United Nations, 16, 62, 73
United States (USA), viii, 4, 5, 8, 9, 11, 16, 24, 35, 56
Universal Declaration of Human Rights, 35
USSR, 13, 14, 15, 19, 20

V

Valencia, 84, 85, 92, 96
variations, 92
Vietnam, 15
violence, 38
vision, 20, 23

W

war, 3, 12, 13, 22, 26
weakness, vii, ix, 11
websites, 34, 49, 60
welfare state, 6, 8, 9
Western countries, 4, 5
Western democratic capitalism, 3, 7
Western Europe, viii, 11, 12, 13, 14, 15, 17, 18, 20, 21, 28, 29, 30, 31, 95, 97
Wolfgang Streeck, 2, 5
workers, 14, 83
world power, vii, viii, ix, 11, 12, 19, 22
World Trade Organization, 2, 36, 65
World Trade Organization (WTO), 2, 36, 65